The Future of Industrial Societies

THE FUTURE OF INDUSTRIAL SOCIETIES

Convergence or Continuing Diversity?

Clark Kerr

Harvard University Press   Cambridge, Massachusetts, and London, England   1983

Copyright © 1983 by the President and Fellows of Harvard College
All rights reserved
Printed in the United States of America
10 9 8 7 6 5 4 3 2 1

This book is printed on acid-free paper, and its binding materials have
been chosen for strength and durability.

LIBRARY OF CONGRESS CATALOGING IN PUBLICATION DATA

Kerr, Clark, 1911–

The future of industrial societies; convergence or continuing diversity?

Bibliography: p.
Includes index.
1. Social history – 1970– . 2. Industrialization –
Social aspects. I. Title.
HN17.5.K47 1983   301   83-146
ISBN 0-674-33850-2

To Frederick H. Harbison, long-time colleague and cherished friend

Preface

THIS BOOK is based on lectures given in Tokyo on May 11, 12, and 13, 1981. They were the fifth in a series of Ishizaka Lectures on "international topics of broad concern," presented under the auspices of Keidanren. The original lectures have been substantially revised.

The subject matter grew out of a research endeavor first undertaken long ago with John T. Dunlop of Harvard, the late Frederick H. Harbison of Princeton (to whom this book is dedicated), and Charles A. Myers of the Massachusetts Institute of Technology. The association with them has been an intellectual and personal experience that I have treasured. Both Dunlop and Myers made many suggestions on the manuscript that have been included here.

Gregory Grossman of the University of California at Berkeley and Frederick L. Pryor of Swarthmore College made most helpful comments during the preparation of the lectures. They shared with me their extensive knowledge of comparative economics, and I am deeply indebted to them for their many suggestions.

Marian Gade and Charlotte Alhadeff assisted me greatly with their research efforts carried out with judgment, careful attention to accuracy, and endless good will toward the many requests directed their way, as they have on other occasions. Maureen Kawaoka managed the manuscript from its nearly illegible beginnings to final completion, and made all the arrangements with Keidanren for the presentation of the lectures—to perfection as always.

C.K.

Contents

Contents

The Future of Industrial Societies

Introduction

HUMAN SOCIETIES historically have been extremely different, one from another. "No animal lives under more diverse conditions than man, and no species exhibits more behavioral variations from one population to the other."[1] This has been the rule for the more than two million years that the human race has been on this planet. The variety of economic activities and of social arrangements among the American Indians of North and South America, for example, has been so immense that it suggests an almost limitless capacity for human ingenuity and adaptability. "The customs and ways of life of Indians in the barrens of Northern Canada . . . had [by the sixteenth century] become totally different from those of Indians who lived along the Atlantic coast, and both had become different in almost all ways from those who lived in deserts in the Southwest, or on islands of the Caribbean, or in other vastly different regions."[2] This variety still exists today in a few remote areas. Humans have spread around the world in all kinds of climates and into all types of natural resource situations, and have adapted to each more creatively than any other living organism. This is one source of their world-wide dominance.

Such historical heterogeneity has clearly been declining as people have left the diverse environments given by nature and created their own environments based initially on sedentary agriculture, then on crafts and commerce, and more recently on industry. They could conceivably have continued to fashion many quite different environments for themselves but instead they have chosen or have been forced by circumstances to concentrate on a few, and in recent times mostly on only one — the modern industrial way of life. As a consequence, "any two or more relatively modernized societies, regardless of variations among them, have more in common with one another at more general structural levels than any one of them has in common with any relatively nonmodernized society."[3]

Does this process of convergence continue once the industrial stage has been reached? Clearly, industrial societies develop in quite different historical, cultural, and resource circumstances. But once established, do they tend to converge in their social arrangements and in their economic performances? Do they all become more or less alike in a process of world-wide homogenization?

There are several possibilities to consider. One is that they do continue to converge. Another is that they continue to reflect, more or less indefinitely, their quite different origins in cultural practices, in ideologies, in leadership groups — that they follow quite diverse, though sometimes parallel, courses of development. Another is that, once industrialized, they increasingly diverge from one another, like an exploding universe, each society following a different trajectory that carries it farther and farther apart from all the others. Still another possibility is that they continue to converge in some aspects but remain different or even diverge in others. Which of these possibilities is the dominant tendency?

I shall use the word *convergence* here to mean the tendency of societies to grow more alike, to develop similarities in structures, processes, and performances. By *divergence* I mean their tendency to recede from one another, to develop greater dissimilarities in structures, processes, and performances. *Uniformity* refers to that state in which societies possess undiversified structures, processes, and performances, and *diversity* to the existence of variety in these elements. Convergence and divergence refer to directions of movement; uniformity and diversity to existing conditions at a moment of time. There may be, of course, many rates of movement in either general direction, and many degrees of uniformity and diversity at any moment of time. The global community might conceivably reach a long-term steady state but such a steady state seems a long way off.

To the extent that there may be a degree of convergence among industrial societies, or at least parallel development, how complete is it? It has been argued by Herbert Marcuse that convergence is total, that the heterogeneity of the past is disappearing into the conformity of what he has called "one-dimensional man" — socially controlled and homogenized, a victim of triumphant technology. "Contemporary industrial society tends to be totalitarian" as a result of both "non-terroristic economic-technical coordination" and "terroristic political coordination."[4] But there are many other possibilities. However complete or incomplete convergence may be in some sectors of society, does it pervade all of society or only some of its parts and in each part to a different degree? What areas, if any, may be exempt?

What are the forces that propel toward or impede convergence? To the extent that there is convergence, what is the direction or directions of its movement? Which of many possible societal forms, if any, becomes the dominant model, or may there be two or more dominant models? To what ultimate or intermediate destination or destinations, if any, is the process directed?

The course of development of industrial society has been a subject for speculation for at least a century and a half, ever since it became clear that a new type of society was being created. The widespread use of the specific term "convergence" is, however, of relatively recent origin. It surfaced around 1960, first in the writings of Jan Tinbergen on "the optimum regime,"[5] and also, quite independently, in a study entitled *Industrialism and Industrial Man* which I wrote in collaboration with John T. Dunlop, Frederick H. Harbison, and Charles A. Myers.[6] The formulation of Tinbergen, contemporaneous with our own, is the more dramatic and widely known. It set forth a point of convergence for industrial societies on "the optimum," whereas we only indicated a range of possibilities broadly defined as "pluralistic industrialism." It tied convergence to the possible realization of a better society for all mankind and even to the prospects for world peace, whereas we limited ourselves to the prediction of continuing social tensions within societies and stopped far short of suggesting a reduction in international tensions. Although less dramatic, our views were, and still are, more realistic about historical trends and about prospects for the future.

In the intervening two decades a great deal has been written on the subject (see the selected bibliography). There are now greatly improved (but still inadequate) statistical data relating to it. And the question of where industrial societies may be tending is once again being actively debated and explored. In the early 1960s the interest in the subject reflected the temporary end of the cold war and the then new tendencies toward the introduction of market mechanisms in socialist countries and of planning in capitalist nations. Currently it reflects intensive efforts at reevaluation of directions in several countries, such as Great Britain, the United States, Poland, and China; and the USSR faces many internal and external stresses at a time when the top leadership is undergoing major changes.[7] It also reflects the new concern about declining rates of economic growth and the possibility of a cessation or even of negative rates of growth, as well as concern about the renewal of the cold war between the superpowers. This, then, seems to be a good time to review the several hypotheses about convergence and to examine the accumulated information that relates to them.

Discussion of convergence hypotheses is one approach to analyzing economic and social developments of the past century and a half in the industrializing world; one way of looking at possible trends in the near future; and one method by which developing nations may seek to anticipate what is likely to happen in the course of their developments and to appraise the choices that may lie before them. These hypotheses (we consider six here) can serve as guides to an understanding of what happens in economic and social development, which factors are the more important to note and to watch, and which directions are being taken or may be taken and why. The guides to be used are a matter of choice: one guide will appeal more to some people than to others; the value of each guide may vary from time to time depending on the circumstances; and some may prefer no guide at all.

How we see the future can decisively affect how we may act today. History has often been forged and is increasingly being forged by visions of the future as well as by legacies of the past — by how we try to fashion our own futures based upon our hopes, our fears, and our expectations. What may we expect in the course of unfolding events? What should we prepare for? What should we try to avoid or to change? Time past and time future, to reverse the phrase of T. S. Eliot, are both contained in time present.

Our focus here will be on already industrialized nations, defined as those with 25 percent or less of the labor force still engaged in agriculture and with relatively high levels of per capita income, and on several additional socialist nations that approximate these conditions. What is happening within and among them? A separate question (to be addressed only briefly) is whether the now industrializing nations will necessarily follow the paths of the already industrialized nations. Karl Marx said that they would: "The country that is more developed industrially only shows, to the less developed, the image of its own future."[8] One of the difficulties with this proposition is that there are today two main models for the future, not one: the socialist or command economy, and the capitalist or market economy. Another difficulty is that there is great variety and constant change within each model; and other major models may come to exist. But it may be said, as Benjamin Ward has, that many nations are now on the "main line" of modernization.[9] And Simon Kuznets has noted the "measurable convergence" between less developed countries and developed countries, including "much convergence in political and ideological aspects."[10] However that series of developments may turn out, our concern here will be largely with the approximately thirty nations already industrialized, according to the definition above, or approaching this definition of industrialization and under socialist direction, and not with the many still industrializing nations and the model or models they may follow or themselves create. In Chapter 3 we will look briefly at the implications of this discussion for nations in the process of becoming industrialized.

I define *industrialism* as a societal form that relies heavily on science and on machine technology; on energy derived from sources other than animals, water and wind; on substantial amounts of saving and investment; on the intensive division of labor and the creation of a formally educated labor force, including many managers and technicians; and on the commercial integration of substantial areas of the planet. These characteristics taken together distinguish industrialism from all former types of economic societies. They have led to great emphasis on ever newer technology, rapid increases in production and productivity, massive shifts of employment from agriculture to industry, urbanization of the population, a revolution in transport and communication, and the establishment of large-scale enterprises, among other results. This definition of industrialism makes no reference to the ownership of property, which can take several forms. Ownership of property is only one of the ways of distinguishing among types of industrialism. Industrialism is the great phenomenon of our age.[11]

The future of industrial societies is a subject that one should approach with great humility. It involves important issues that are extremely complex and extremely varied; and the social and economic context of world society is changing rapidly. No one can know for sure what is now happening, let alone what will happen. This is an area of controversy where there can be judgments based on observation and analysis, but no sense of absolute assurance — and judgments differ. I present my judgments in the spirit of suppositions that have not yet been proved.

The suppositions that people hold can have an impact on current analysis and conduct, even on the conduct of foreign policy as between the two superpowers. The United States secretary of state, George Shultz, in a speech on October 18, 1982, stated in part: "Recent developments in countries under communist rule also suggest that a new age of democratic reform and revolution lies ahead of us. The weaknesses of communist societies are becoming increasingly apparent. Popular desires for freedom remain strong. The concessions that communist regimes make to popular sentiment and to economic necessity may sow the seeds of their transformation."[12]

The foreign policy of the other great superpower — the USSR — is, by contrast, based at least partly on the conviction that it is capitalism which, in the words of Marx and Engels, sows the seeds of its own, not transformation, but "destruction," that produces its own "gravediggers."

These contrary suppositions about the directions of convergence may well set the dynamics for some of the future of the world. But they are not the only suppositions that might guide analysis and conduct.

Laws of Motion
of Industrial Societies

1   KARL MARX was certain that there is an "economic law of motion of modern society" that governs its "normal development" and declared that his "ultimate aim" was to "lay bare" this law. His special concern was with the "successive phases" that modern societies must go through — in particular, with the ultimate destination of modern society, which he saw as convergence on second-phase socialism or communism. The law he thought he had identified worked, he believed, with "iron necessity towards inevitable results."[1]

     Not only Marx but also Joseph Schumpeter, that great proponent of the role of the private entrepreneur in the development of modern society, saw elemental forces at work: "Mankind is not free to choose . . . Things economic and social move by their own momentum and the ensuing situations compel individuals and groups to behave in certain ways whatever they may wish to do."[2]

The possible existence and the nature of such laws of motion have been of interest to many others besides Marx and Schumpeter. Following is a small selection of the many views on this subject.

Six Competing and Contradictory Laws of Motion

Convergence on Christian industrialism. One of the first people to examine the inherent logic of industrial society was Henri Saint-Simon, who wrote in the first quarter of the nineteenth century. He was extremely perceptive about the new type of society that was just emerging in England and France. He thought the process then underway would continue until the world was "totally industrialized" in "every land." It was to be the "final system" in all history. Social classes would rise and fall in the course of this transition, but society would in the end be "governed by an educated elite." The workers, however, would have great influence, which would require "a policy by which the proletariat will have the strongest interest in maintaining public order." This would necessitate, among other things, "ensuring work for all fit men." The new society would be based on the "progress of ideas" and would require "spreading . . . knowledge" to all the people. A central purpose of public policy would come to be "to afford all members of society the greatest possible opportunity for the development of their faculties," and each individual would draw "benefits from society in exact proportion . . . to the beneficent use he makes of his abilities." This would be an "organic society," internally consistent, that would converge on "Christian industrialism" which would combine economic efficiency with high moral concern for distributive justice.[3]

Here, early on, were ideas, later more fully developed by others, that foresaw the triumph of industrialization, the rise to a position of influence of what came to be identified by John Kenneth Galbraith as the "technostructure,"[4] the inevitable influence of the workers in what was called by Sumner Slichter the "laboristic state,"[5] and the importance of policies of full employment, universal education, equality of opportunity, pay according to ability, building a social consensus, and creating a welfare state.

I have given first attention to Saint-Simon because of his early insistence that there was a consistent logic to the development of industrial society, his insight as to the components of that logic, and his belief (perhaps the earliest in history) that there was a point of final convergence for all industrial societies. His view of what was then the future, now seen from the vantage point of a century and a half later, is still a good portrait of some important aspects of several modern industrial societies. It stands, unsurpassed for its time, as a perceptive portrait of the economic society of the future, as do the writings of Alexis de Tocqueville on the emerging democratic political society. Tocqueville, in the political realm, saw a convergence on social mobility and on equality.[6]

Convergence on communism. Karl Marx also saw a final point of convergence for society and a process by which this uniformity would be reached. I take a "hard" view of Marx on economic determinism and not the "soft" view of Engels.[7] In this respect, I agree with the position of G. A. Cohen in his book *Karl Marx's Theory of History.*[8] Some soft, and apologetic, views of Marx end up as intellectual mush — with everything affecting and being affected by everything else.

The final point of convergence for Marx was communism. He never spelled it out in any detail; but in this second or higher phase of socialism, the ownership of property will have been socialized, the class stratification of people will have disappeared, the state (as he defined it) will have "withered away," the economy will be managed by a "free and equal association of producers," there will be universal affluence, people will choose what they want to do ("hunt in the morning, fish in the afternoon, rear cattle in the evening, criticize after dinner, just as I have a mind") and they will work according to their ability and be paid according to their need.[9] The system will ultimately be world wide.[10]

At the center of human society, for Marx, was the "organization of production and distribution" in the economy, as Leon Trotsky later observed.[11] Marx was very farsighted when he predicted the central role of energy in the evolution of society. "In acquiring new productive forces men change their mode of production, and in changing their mode of production, in changing the way of earning their living, they change all their social relations. The windmill gives you society with the feudal lord; the steammill, society with the industrial capitalist."[12] He did not live to see the development of energy from oil, or from the atom.

Once capitalism had been created on the basis of the "steam-mill," Marx believed that it would progress not through evolution, as with Saint-Simon, but generally through revolution by the workers into the subsequent "dictatorship of the proletariat" of first-phase socialism. "The transition from one system to another was always determined by the growth of productive forces, i.e., of techniques and the organization of labor." "At the base of society is not religion and morality but nature and labor"; and "existence" determines "consciousness," not the other way around.[13] The "economic base structure" relates to the means of existence and the "superstructure" to the resulting consciousness, with the superstructure determined or at least strongly influenced by the economic base structure. Thus, there is a consistency in society, except during periods of transition when contradictions do arise, with material productive forces determining the relations of production among men, even "independent of their will." On these relations "rise legal and political superstructures, . . . to which correspond definite forms of social consciousness."[14] This means that with similar productive forces, there will develop similar economic and political and social and ideological systems. In particular, capitalist societies were all thought to be alike in almost all of their aspects, although possible exceptions were expressed for evolutionary, rather than revolutionary, changes in some nations; specifically mentioned were England, the United States, and Holland. The processes of capitalist development, for Marx, were highly similar, if not entirely identical; but the ultimate end result was always the same — the extinction of capitalism.

Marx's vision of the law of motion of modern society has politically animated many leaders in many parts of the world. The leaders of nations now possessing one-third of the population of the world generally subscribe to it, at least officially; for them, this is the declared immutable law of modern history.

There have been many interpretations, defenses and criticisms of Marx. There have also been many non-Marxist social scientists who have agreed with Marx on one point or another. I select only one of these for mention because he was so astute an observer of social life: Thorstein Veblen. He emphasized the all-pervasive influence of "machine technology" that leads workers to "materialistic" and "socialistic" convictions — "work shapes the habits of thought" to the extent that people who work the same way will think the same way.[15]

Convergence on capitalism. I once took a course at the London School of Economics from F. A. Hayek entitled "Collectivist Economic Planning," a subject on which he had recently published a book.[16] His argument was that collectivist planning could not work, that central planning would seriously impair productivity, and that efforts at achieving equality of earned income would drastically reduce incentives. Socialist planning could lead only to "economic decay," since it is so "incredibly clumsy, primitive and limited in scope." Capitalism would bury socialism. Hayek also believed that any combination of democracy with socialism was "unachievable." "There is no other possibility than either the order governed by the impersonal discipline of the market or that directed by the will of a few individuals; and those who are out to destroy the first are wittingly or unwittingly helping to create the second."[17] If you destroyed the market, he thought, you also destroyed democracy.

Hayek reserved time at the end of the last lecture for questions. The first was: "Professor Hayek, do you believe you have proved that a planned economy cannot possibly work?" Hayek replied, "I may not have proved it to you, but I absolutely believe it to be true"; and he abruptly left the lecture hall, subsequently entering many others around the world with the same message.

W. W. Rostow was less blunt about it, in his *Stages of Economic Growth,* but it is clear that he thought that the USSR would have a very difficult time moving from the stage of economic "maturity" to the final stage of the "age of high mass consumption." High mass consumption involves very complex decision making and great attention to the desires of individual consumers. To the extent, however, that the USSR might enter this stage, it would, in effect, become Americanized. Rostow described communism as "a disease of the transition" — a disease that resulted from the early absence of the necessary preconditions for a smooth economic transition to modern industrial society. He did not suggest that the disease was fatal, but it was certainly serious. Thus, the subtitle of his book was "A Non-Communist Manifesto." The world of the future clearly belonged to capitalism.[18]

Convergence on the optimum. In the 1950s Khrushchev replaced Stalin. Market socialism and worker control of enterprises was being developed in Yugoslavia. The West was moving rapidly into welfare-state capitalism and experimenting with some macro- and even micro-economic planning, as in France. Newly industrializing countries all over the world were trying out mixed economies. The cold war was temporarily abating and with it some of the intensity of the ideological rhetoric. It was natural to ask whether societies around the world might not end up very much alike, having, by trial and error, come to the same solutions to common problems.

Jan Tinbergen published a paper in 1959 on what he called "the theory of the optimum regime," a theme which he and his followers later elaborated on several occasions. Tinbergen noted that "economic regimes of whatever kind have, to a considerable degree, common tasks and objectives." These tasks and objectives include seeking to maximize the welfare of the people today and establishing an optimum rate of growth into the future. The two major means of achieving these results are the market and the state plan. Tinbergen felt that the market was inherently better at making decisions where there were decreasing returns to scale and no substantial external effects of the process; and that the state was the better decision maker where there were increasing returns to scale leading to monopolies and where substantial social costs or benefits had to be taken into account. He also believed that the state was inherently better than the market at assuring law and order, managing the supply of money, providing roads and education facilities, handling taxation, and redistributing income, among other societal functions. In the search for optimum methods to obtain optimum results, he foresaw a mixed system, "not some form of extreme."

Thus he visualized "converging ideas rather than diverging" and thought that, to the extent that "there really is a more or less clearly defined optimum regime, actual regimes will have to move toward the optimum;" and he clearly thought there was such an optimum. He feared that any "concentration of political views around the opposite poles" would advance "the process toward self-annihilation." Peace depended on convergence.[19]

What might hold up this process of convergence that advanced both individual human welfare and international peace? Tinbergen suggested four obstacles: "doctrinaire" opinions, "misunderstandings" of economic relationships, "short-sighted" actions that ignore future well-being, and the absence of a political system with intelligent and responsive leaders. The enemies of human welfare and peace were rigid ideologies, poor economic analysis, selfish behavior, and inadequate governance — powerful but not unconquerable enemies, in practice.

Tinbergen thought that, in fact, the East and West had both changed "profoundly" and had moved toward each other. Each side had learned from its own experiences and also from the other.[20] What was mostly needed, in the words of Andrzej Brzeski, was "intelligent social engineering by a benevolent bureaucracy" in order to enter the chosen world of Tinbergen.[21] The "best of possible worlds," to use a phrase of Voltaire, is there for the taking. Convergence serves individuals, nations, and the world.

The Tinbergen approach can even be used to describe all of human history around the world as a great search for and the subsequent spread of better productive techniques and better systems of social organization — the age-long piecemeal discovery and dissemination of optimum, or at least better, ways of doing things. This may be viewed as the eternal quest of mankind and the central theme of history. This is the approach taken by William H. McNeill in his *Rise of the West*.[22] History is written around the centers of initiative from which new ideas and methods have spread, centers such as the Middle East in the ancient world and Western Europe, the United States, Russia, Japan, and China in the modern world. The center of the world is wherever the best new ideas and courses of action are being born and developed; all the rest is peripheral or even nonconsequential.

Andrei Sakharov, Russian physicist and winner of the Nobel Prize for Peace, began his concern for convergence out of fear of world-wide nuclear destruction. Convergence is essential to survival. Also, it serves national needs. The Soviet system, in particular, he believed, needs to liberalize itself internally in order to move forward. He said that in "achieving a high productivity of social labor or developing all productive forces or ensuring a high standard of living for most of the population, capitalism and socialism seem to have 'played to a tie.'" He added, however, that in the more advanced, scientifically based industries, the USSR was now falling behind because of its more secretive, bureaucratic methods of management. He wanted a greater role for the market. "Capitalists" have learned to use "the social principles of socialism" and socialists should now also learn from capitalism. The two systems should learn from each other. This, incidentally, echoes a comment of Marx that "one nation can and should learn from others."[23] "Both capitalism and socialism," Sakharov wrote, "are capable of long-term development, borrowing positive elements from each other, and actually coming closer to each other in a number of essential aspects." Having converged, they could then better help solve, together, the great problems of the world, leading to "the creation of a world government."

He noted that the Soviet Union and the United States were going through "the same course of increasing complexity of structure, . . . giving rise in both countries to managerial groups that are similar in social character." And he said that "there is no qualitative difference in the structure of society of the two countries in terms of distribution of consumption."

Above all, Sakharov believed that coexistence, based in part on convergence, was a necessity of the modern world. "More important, the facts suggest that on any other course except ever-increasing coexistence and collaboration between the two systems and the two superpowers, with a smoothing of contradictions and with mutual assistance, on any other course annihilation awaits mankind. There is no other way out."[24]

Convergence on the pragmatic. Related to the idea of the attraction of the optimum is the view that, in the end, pragmatic solutions will prevail — what works perhaps not best but at least better in each situation. Often what works best or better will be the same in several societies, but it may be that what works best or better depends on the conditions of a particular society. The essence of this view is not that there is only one best way, although sometimes there may be, but that the basic test is results — which cats, regardless of color, catch the most mice in each particular situation.

In the period 1955–1965 there was in Western Europe and the United States much talk about the end of ideology. In 1955 Raymond Aron published an essay called "The End of the Ideological Age?" and this essay was the origin of the phrase.[25] But there were precursors going back at least as far as Max Weber, who wrote of the decline of the importance of ideology with the rise of what he called "functional rationality."[26] Karl Mannheim in his *Ideology and Utopia* said that societies were moving more toward the practical and away from the utopian.[27] Bertrand Russell was another early exponent of this view: "the practical difference between capitalism and socialism is not so great as politicians on both sides suppose."[28]

The American group that adopted this view included Daniel Bell, John Kenneth Galbraith, Seymour Martin Lipset, Talcott Parsons, David Riesman, Arthur Schlesinger, Jr., and Edward Shils; the European group included Bertrand de Jouvenel, Isaiah Berlin, Ralf Dahrendorf, and Maurice Duverger.

The central theme was the rise of practical considerations in the making of economic and social policy. A subsidiary theme was that the new conditions of production required more freedom for individuals in thought and discourse, and in the political life of nations, than socialist systems had in the past permitted. Schlesinger wrote that "the choice between private and public means . . . is simply a practical question as to which means can best achieve the desired end" and added that we should "banish the words 'capitalism' and 'socialism' from intellectual discourse."[29] Galbraith said that the "nature of technology — the nature of the large organization that it sustains, and the nature of planning that technology requires — has an importance of its own and this is causing a greater convergence in all industrial societies;" and "in fewer years than we imagine, this will produce a rather indistinguishable melange of planning and market influences." This would lead in turn to greater political and cultural freedom because "deep scientific perception and deep technical specialization cannot be reconciled with intellectual regimentation."[30] He expected convergence between socialism and capitalism at "all fundamental points" and said this "will dispose of the notion of inevitable conflict based on irreconcilable difference."[31]

The presumption among at least some members of the group was that societies would converge on a mixture of guided capitalism and democratic socialism, or what Lipset called "conservative socialism."[32] Many of the group later backed away from the stronger versions of "end of ideology," and Lipset in 1977 said that all that was meant was that the most "passionate attachments" to revolutionary ideologies, right and left, were diminishing.[33]

The "end of ideology" theme may be said to have been a temporary intellectual fad based upon the relaxation of the cold war, the experiments with the market in the East and with the economic plan in the West, and the hope for world peace. But it was more than that. There was at the center of the theory the perception that ideologies do not go on forever unchanged, that practical considerations sometimes override ideology, that new generations of leaders find their own ways to determine and to justify what they are doing.

Convergence on pluralistic industrialism. In 1960 Dunlop,

Harbison, Myers, and I published *Industrialism and Industrial Man*.[34] It was concerned specifically with the evolution of industrial relations systems within economies, but it also set forth a theory of partial convergence. The book represented an effort to break away from the ethnocentric orientation of studies of industrial relations in the United States; to provide an alternative view to those of Marx, the Webbs, and John R. Commons on the evolution of industrial relations systems; and, also, to challenge the dogma that capitalism and socialism were in all respects totally different and that they were necessarily deadly enemies — a reaction to both Joseph McCarthy and Joseph Stalin.

Industrialism was set forth as having a logic of its own, whether under capitalism or socialism or other auspices. Much of what happens to management and to labor is the same regardless of auspices. This logic of industrialism requires four things.

First, the creation of an industrial work force which must be recruited, committed, advanced in its skills, and maintained in a state of productivity. The work force must be mobile geographically and occupationally, must be educated, and must be given a structure of rules within which to work.

Second, the establishment of large-scale production enterprises and large cities, and the creation of a substantial role for government and of a workable consensus about what should and should not be done.

Third, the development of a leadership group with policies that make at least adequate use of the available productive resources. These leadership groups all face somewhat the same range of choices to be made and decisions to be taken. Managers of productive enterprises, whether public or private, play key roles, and they are increasingly professionals, highly trained and advanced on merit.

Fourth, the evolution of a work force that comes to accept the economic structure. This acceptance is based on sharing the gains of industrialism, on sharing influence at least over workplace rules, on obtaining a degree of security on and off the job. The work force becomes integrated with the community and more dedicated to evolutionary than to revolutionary change, whether under capitalism or socialism.

Industrial society converges on what we called *pluralistic industrialism*, a type of society in which power (or at least influence) is shared formally or informally by political leaders, however chosen; by managers, whether of state or of private enterprises; by workers, whose consent must be obtained by contract or by assent on the job; and even by intellectuals and by trained professionals. We saw the system as always moving, always changing, never reaching a final equilibrium. We contrasted pluralistic industrialism with societies based on unitary or monolithic (command) or atomistic (market) ideologies and practices. Groups and group interests come to play major parts along with the central state or with autonomous individuals; clusters of individuals come to have substantial power or at least some independent influence. Pure state socialism and pure atomistic competition are both modified in the direction of the multiple sharing of power and influence by the state, by individuals, and by intermediate groups. We saw the growth of a tripartite (the state, management, organized labor) constitutionalism (the "web of rules") in industrial relations and in the relations of production more generally, with leaders in each of the three sectors in a strong role of influence.

There was, we thought, no one route to the future and no single destination but rather a substantial range of possibilities and no utopia ever. We challenged what we considered to be the simplistic view, then widely current, of two totally different, totally unchanging systems forever facing each other. We suggested, instead, that there were several intermediate and changing solutions between the two extremes; instead of pure capitalism versus pure socialism, there were several mutating forms of pluralistic industrialism in various relations to one another. The future lay with a diversity of economic arrangements rather than with any single uniformity or with opposing dual uniformities.

I later treated this same question in *Marshall, Marx and Modern Times*.[35] I referred to the "multidimensional society" that had several or even many centers of power and influence, and where the ideology of class conflict fades away but where new ideologies concerning new patterns of life are being born; and I noted particularly the new demand for what I called multiple-option lives. Within pluralistic industrialism, I identified four kinds of arrangements, for illustrative purposes: (1) coordinated pluralism, (2) managerial pluralism, (3) liberal pluralism, and (4) syndicalism. The first gives a strong role (but not totalitarian control of state enterprises) to central authority, the second to managers of decentralized private organizations including unions, the third to individual choice and influence both outside and within groups, and the fourth to self-governing work units within the framework of state authority. I now prefer to identify the first as "decentralized socialism" or, to use the phrase of Alec Nove, "centralized pluralism";[36] the second as "coordinated capitalism" or "decentralized pluralism"; and the last as "state-directed syndicalism," as in Yugoslavia. The third, "liberal pluralism," is a version of pluralism with a "human face."[37] Neither the state nor the market solely and totally rules supreme in any of these illustrative economic systems. The state, the intermediate organization, and the individual all have influence; no one element is fully dominant. There is a great spectrum of actual and possible pluralistic solutions.

Thus, we see from the above examples that theoreticians have formulated widely varying theories of convergence: that it results from the application of social principles, essentially religious in origin, to the use of the new means of production (Saint-Simon); that it results from scientific laws governing social change (Marx); that it results from the clear superiority of market mechanisms (Hayek); that it evolves from efforts to find the optimum way of doing things (Tinbergen); that it is the consequence of a declining role for ideology and a rise of pragmatism ("end of ideology" school); and that it is happening among different systems facing the same sets of problems and working out a variety of pluralistic solutions in the course of facilitating production ("industrialism and industrial man" group). For Marx and Hayek, convergence, or "submergence,"[38] was a necessity of social life; for Saint-Simon and Tinbergen, a desirable outcome of man's perfectionist quest for a better world; and for the "end of ideology" school and the "industrialism and industrial man" group, an evolutionary and pragmatic result of contending social forces.

Theories of Convergence in Key Aspects of Societies

The approaches discussed above all set forth a course of convergence covering several, or even many, aspects of society. In addition, there have been suggestions of convergence in one particular and very important facet of society but not in the totality of society.

On bureaucracy and rationalization. For Max Weber, "the primary source of the superiority of bureaucratic administration lies in the role of technical knowledge which, through the development of modern technology and business methods in the production of goods, has become completely indispensable. In this respect, it makes no difference whether the economic system is organized on a capitalistic or a socialistic basis." "The future belongs to bureaucratization."[39] The socialist society would, of course, be more bureaucratic than the capitalist society because of its emphasis on the plan. Talcott Parsons also argued that rationalization through the use of technical knowledge required a central role for bureaucracy.[40] Maria Hirszowicz wrote of the "sovereign bureaucracy" in the USSR.[41]

On planning. For John Kenneth Galbraith, the convergence is on planning. "The modern large corporation and the modern apparatus of socialist planning are variant combinations of the same need . . . There is no tendency for the Soviet and Western systems to convergence by the return of the former to the market. Both have outgrown that. There is measurable convergence to the same form of planning . . . The technostructure in the cases of both public and private ownership assumes similar powers and uses the same group methods for arriving at decisions . . . Given the decision to have modern industry, much of what happens is inevitable and the same . . . Thereafter the imperatives of organization, technology and planning operate similarly, and we have seen to a broadly similar result, on all societies."[42]

On the centrality of managers. James Burnham wrote that "at the conclusion of the transition period the managers will, in fact, have achieved social dominance, will be the ruling class in society. This drive, moreover, is world-wide in extent." There was to be managerial capitalism and managerial socialism.[43] Peter Drucker once wrote, in reference to Western capitalism, that "management as it emerged during the last generation is the new ruling group in our society," and "its politics and principles determine very largely the character of our society."[44] David Granick has concluded about the USSR that "well trained, well disciplined, politically conscious and active, the Red Executive seems a figure permanently established in the seats of the mighty."[45] Harbison and Myers also noted how managers come to play a more central role in industrial society and emphasized how they tended to evolve from "patrimonial management" in capitalism and "political management" in socialism to "professional management" in both systems.[46]

Opposition and Doubts

Marxists. The Russian establishment has been totally opposed to recent Western convergence hypotheses. It lumps together all the various theories of convergence advanced by intellectuals in Western Europe and the United States under the one theme of the alleged movement of socialism and capitalism toward each other. It claims to expect, instead, the world-wide triumph of its form of socialism — the type of convergence that Marx envisioned. The doctrine of two-way convergence is seen as a source of corruption for students and intellectuals (as in the case of Sakharov) in Russia, and for leaders and potential leaders in developing countries. A study of Russian reactions by Leon Gouré and associates concludes: "It will come as no surprise to anyone who is aware of the implications for the basic tenets of Marxism-Leninism that to the Soviet leadership the very thought of any possible convergence of the socialist and capitalist systems is simply and strictly anathema. Every theory and argument put forward in the West that lends itself to the direct or indirect support of any such idea is denounced from the highest to the lowest levels of the vast theoretical and propaganda apparatus of the Soviet Union. The very development of the convergence concept . . . is treated as a new but highly virulent manifestation of 'anti-communism' which has as its purpose undermining the Soviet system, sowing discord between the USSR and other socialist countries, stifling the 'liberation' movements of the Third World, and dulling class consciousness of the masses in advanced Western countries."[47] One article on the subject is entitled "Tactics of the Doomed" and calls the thesis of convergence "ideological subversion." It claims, in particular, that the thesis ignores "the difference between social and political structures, taking into consideration only the level of industrialization."[48]

Soviet-oriented Marxists in Western Europe, the United States, and Japan have echoed the Russian position. There have been exceptions among other Marxists, however. Paul Sweezy in 1971 quoted with approval a Chinese criticism of Russian communism which said the "the forces of capitalism run wild in town and countryside" in Russia. He added: "It is noteworthy that the foregoing characterization of the situation in the Soviet Union could be applied with little or no change to almost any capitalist country, the main difference being that under capitalism a large part of the activities alluded to are perfectly legal."[49] Russian communism was converging on capitalism. Wlodzimierz Brus, now but not in earlier times a self-styled "reformist Marxist," wrote in 1977, based particularly on his Polish orientation, that "divergences between the two systems have become in practice palpably smaller" and that the "converging elements could become even stronger," but he thinks it "perilous" to support some ultimate "point of convergence."[50]

Non-Marxists. Non-Marxist doubters, critics, and opponents have advanced many objections to the theses of convergence. One of these is *historical determinism*, according to which history perpetuates itself and is not easily overridden.

Joseph Schumpeter, who expected a mild form of creeping socialism to emerge out of capitalism, wrote, however, that "social structures, types and attitudes are coins that do not readily melt. Once they are formed they persist, possibly for centuries," and "national behavior" will "more or less depart from what we should expect it to be if we tried to infer it from the dominant forms of the productive process." He noted, nevertheless, that "any rational behavior must of course display certain formal similarities with any other rational behavior."[51] This historical determinism, in the words of Bertram Wolfe, means that "every land moves toward its future in terms of its own past, its own institutions and traditions."[52] Wolfe, by the 1960s a self-styled "exceptionalist," argued that there are exceptions "for all the lands of the earth," each "under the influence of its own heritage, its traditions and its institutions," and that each land was "conserved and altered more by the actions of men than by the weight of things." Echoing the fears of the Russian establishment, but from the opposite end of the political spectrum, he believes that "there is mischief as well as error in the convergence theory," for it can result in losing "our perspective on what is worth defending in our society." In particular, he is critical of the "end of ideology" views of Galbraith.[53]

A second objection is *ideological determinism*, which argues that leaders often believe their ideologies, act upon them, and perpetuate them. Zbigniew Brzezinski has noted the powerful impact of ideology on the conduct of the Soviet system but has acknowledged that it is subject to some "erosion over time."[54] Alexander Gerschenkron, a careful student of Russian history, concludes that ideology is most likely to be influential in the early stages of industrialization, as were the theories of Saint-Simon in the first half of the nineteenth century in France. The relative importance of ideology, in fact, reflects "the degree of backwardness" of the nation; and, as time goes on, ideology becomes less of a force. Specifically, there have been "important processes of change in Soviet ideology" and ideology is now used more "in order to justify policies which are pursued for eminently practical reasons that have little to do with Marxian theories and beliefs."[55]

Nevertheless, in certain societies at certain times in history, ideology does play a major part. It excludes some types of action and concentrates attention on others. And it may even be said that "all individuals have ideology" all of the time, if one defines a commitment to certain basic values as an ideology.[56] However, some ideologies are more explicit or more all-encompassing or both than are others.

A third non-Marxist theory against convergence is *teleological determinism*. Rationality might lead to similar methods and results if all societies had similar "goals, beliefs, and values," but they do not. Different ends require different means; so do different beliefs and different values. Thus, although "common processes of rationalization, and their interplay, will yield somewhat common, or at least comparable, results," there can be no "common destination." This is the central argument of Wilbert Moore.[57]

Fourth, some non-Marxists oppose convergence on the basis of *bimodal polarity*. Two or more solutions may be equally viable, and no one solution may be so superior as to drive out others. Frederic L. Pryor concludes that "the performance differences between systems do not appear to be great," in his review "of economic performance of nations with greater and less centralization." "There does not appear to be any hard scientific evidence, either empirical or theoretical, that unambiguously points to the economic desirability of a high or low degree of centralization." He concludes, at least tentatively, that "mixed economies" tend to be "unstable" and to lack "coherence," thus tending to "move either toward more centralized or decentralized property patterns." Additionally, "when faced with trade-offs between individual freedom and individual equality," it is not "at all clear" that "all nations would make the same choice." And since "economic, political, and social systems in all nations are profoundly conservative in the sense that all contain strong mechanisms for their own continuance," they tend to continue whatever they are doing. He notes that in neither the East nor the West has there been any radical change in property ownership or any radical change in centralization and decentralization.[58] He sees a relatively static bimodal distribution of economic systems.

Who Has Been Right and Who Has Been Wrong?

In looking back over the various views of convergence set forth above, what can we say in a preliminary way about their relative validity?

Saint-Simon was certainly most perceptive about some of the tendencies in industrialism, but he did not foresee the possiblity of a more or less monolithic socialist mode of industrialism.

Marx was right about the possibility of first-phase socialism, but he was wrong in his belief that it would universally evolve out of mature capitalism; to date, it has not. He was also wrong in thinking that second-phase socialism, or communism, would follow first-phase socialism; it has not. This continues to be an embarrassment to socialist nations. Lenin early realized this and wrote about "higher stage or phase" socialism that "no one has ever promised, or even thought to 'introduce', because, generally speaking, it cannot be 'introduced.'" Presumably it might some day evolve, but the Communist Party, Lenin argued, could not be held guilty of not having introduced it. Lenin also explained that "the state withers away [only] in so far as there are no longer any capitalists, any classes, and consequently, no *class* can be *suppressed*."[59] This has left socialism at the level of first-phase, "dictatorship of the proletariat" socialism, with the Communist Party considering itself to be representative of the proletariat and with a strong state apparatus, and without realization of such other promises as "to each according to his need" and an end to the division of labor. And capitalism has survived.

Hayek, too, was wrong. Planned economies likewise could survive, and they have survived, with some help from market mechanisms. To the question "Can socialism work?" Schumpeter answered, "Of course it can."[60] And it has. And laissez-faire capitalism, so favored by Hayek, has given way everywhere to adulterated forms.

Tinbergen was partly correct: all industrial societies have found that some at least minimum mixture of decision making by the state and by the market works best. But he was wrong in areas where there is no optimum solution because of different goals or different values and beliefs. And he was wrong in thinking that even if there is an optimum solution, people will pursue it diligently: they may or they may not – the efficiency of the pursuit may vary enormously. Tinbergen also underestimated the role of vested-interest groups in obstructing the general welfare. Tinbergen and his colleagues later limited convergence only to "economic aspects" of society and left "as open questions (1) whether ideological positions are being depolarized and (2) whether political accommodation between the two blocs can be achieved" – in other words, whether convergence leads to common political structures and to peace. "But it remains important to state that the foundations of both 'Stalinist' and capitalist views are being gradually undermined."[61]

One of Tinbergen's colleagues, J. van den Doel, set forth a theory of partial convergence in amendment to Tinbergen (as explained by Michael Ellman).[62] Doel accepted the view that "different economic systems have different objectives"; thus, they tend to converge to an appreciable extent but not in their totality, since pursuit of different goals holds them partially apart (see Figure 1.1). Ellman criticized even this limited convergence theory, noting that any nation, in the absence of adequate knowledge and in the midst of internal political conflict, would have difficulty maximizing any fixed set of goals. He noted also the varying availability of resources and the differing nature of social constraints in the environments that surround different nations, even if they have the same or similar goals. The concept of an optimum, or of alternative optima, is an elusive one.

The "end of ideology" group was probably correct in saying that pragmatism gains as societies mature, but it was never very specific about what was pragmatic. Dictatorship by the Communist Party may, for example, be the pragmatic solution from the point of view of its leaders in a socialist society. Certainly the group went too far when some of its members suggested that "capitalism" and "socialism" were outdated concepts.

The "industrialism and industrial man" group was wrong in

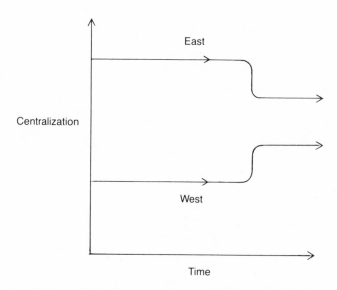

Figure 1.1. Doel's theory of partial convergence.

suggesting that the industrial mode of production would so quickly and so completely conquer the world and so overwhelmingly impose its own cultural patterns on preexisting cultures; industrialism does conquer and it does impose, but less rapidly and less totally than we implied, and we later modified our views.[63] We were correct in suggesting that the range of actual economic structures would narrow to those that could be identified as pluralistic, but we should have clarified that we were not necessarily implying the parallel development of pluralistic political structures. We should have made clear that we were talking essentially about economic and not about political pluralism. The term "industrial" before pluralism implied this but we never stated this directly, in part because we were writing specifically about industrial relations and "productive activities" and not about societies in their entireties. I continue to agree strongly, however, with our view that future convergence would not occur on any single uniform and fixed economic structure, and that conflict and change would go on forever. We saw no linear flow of history in accordance with any single principle or force leading to a set-in-advance result. We were not determinists. We envisioned a perpetual ebb and flow of conflicting forces and of differing social arrangements: "The threads of diversity and the sources of uniformity have been in conflict and they will continue to be, certainly, for many decades and possibly even centuries ahead."[64] We suggested no single optimum solution as did Tinbergen, but rather a range of viable solutions; and we recognized that what was pragmatic in one set of conditions and for one group of people might not be pragmatic under other conditions and for other groups of people. Thus, a range of types of societies might continue to exist even if they were all "pragmatically" managed.

Analyses of key new developments in industrial society, whether the growth of bureaucracy (Weber), a new centrality for planning (Galbraith), or a dominant position for enterprise managers (Burnham), can be helpful in illuminating what is happening; but in each case, of necessity, there is a tendency to overemphasize the particular development under discussion to the neglect of much else that is happening. The role of each new development must be evaluated within a broader framework. This same comment applies to objections to convergence theories based on the tenacity of history, the holding power of ideologies, or the legitimacy of contrasting goals. Each, by itself, is a force at work; but each must be viewed in the light of concurrent events. None is solely in command of the situation—not history, not ideology, not chosen goals. Tunnel vision that sees only one development or one force neglects much of the complex social landscape.

I have come to be more sympathetic with the bipolar solution of Pryor, particularly for the two superpowers engaged in a great military, economic, and ideological confrontation. Some of the lesser powers, however, seem to be more free to experiment and to change. I note, in particular, that the most mixed capitalist societies, Sweden and Japan, have also most prospered in recent decades—that these mixed economies have not proved to be particularly "unstable," although each has its own problems. The same might be said, on the other

Table 1.1. Schematic outline of theories of convergence.

Scope of convergence		Direction of movement	
Full or partial	Sphere	One-way	Two-way or multiway
Full	Economic and political spheres of society	To communism: Marx To capitalism: Hayek	To Christian industrialism: Saint-Simon To the optimum: Tinbergen
Full	Some specified sphere	To central role for bureaucracy: Weber To utilization of planning: Galbraith To managerial dominance: Burnham and Drucker	
Partial	Economic and political spheres		To the pragmatic: "end of ideology" group
Partial	Economic sphere		To pluralistic industrialism: "industrialism and industrial man" group

Note: This presentation draws on an earlier paradigm in E. C. Dunning and E. I. Hopper, "Industrialism and the Problem of Convergence," *Sociological Review*, n.s. 14 (July 1966): 163–186.

Table 1.2. Dynamic outline of theories of convergence: projected directions of movement.

Proponent	East	West
(1) Marx	Communism • ←———————————	
(2) Hayek	——————————————→ • Capitalism	
(3) Saint-Simon	Christian industrialism (economic efficiency and distributive justice) ———→ • ←———	
(4) Tinbergen	The optimum regime ———→ |Current and future welfare of the people| ←———	
(5) "End of ideology" group	Pragmatic range of solutions ———→ |Including guided capitalism and democratic socialism| ←———	
(6) "Industrialism and industrial man" group	Solutions within range of pluralistic industrialism in the economic sphere ——→ |Including pluralistic socialism, pluralistic capitalism and state syndicalism| ←——	
(7) Pryor	Bimodal polarity Centralized systems | ←—— ——→ | Decentralized systems	

Note: (1) and (2) and (3) are static equilibrium solutions: once reached, they will continue unchanged in a static harmony. (4) and (5) are dynamic equilibrium solutions: once reached, they will keep on adjusting to new conditions but each time returning to an equilibrium. (6) is a dynamic solution with movements back and forth within a wide but not unlimited range of possibilities in an evolutionary dissonance. (7) is a dynamic convergence toward two relatively stable but contrasting solutions.

side of the great divide, of Hungary and Yugoslavia: they, too, have mixed economies and are not particularly "unstable."

A summary view of this discussion is provided by schematic and dynamic outlines of the selected theories of convergence (see Tables 1.1 and 1.2). These outlines again make the point that there are many theories of convergence — that a person cannot take a position for or against "convergence theory" as though it were a single entity. Convergence theories vary enormously.

Some critics have aggregated theories of convergence to an excessive degree; they combine not only the unlike but even absolute opposites, and accuse all such theories of being utopian or economically determinist or historicist whether they are or not. It is important to recognize the great variety of hypotheses that come under the heading of convergence, to treat each hypothesis as a separate entity, to note the extent of coverage of each hypothesis. On the last point, for example, I have recently been identified as a "true believer in convergence"[65] (a dreadful sin, according to some) on the sole grounds of a citation to an article I once wrote on the necessity confronting all industrializing nations to commit a labor force to industrial life — what I called the "inevitability of commitment."[66] Convergence on the means to achieve a committed industrial labor force is a long way from convergence on some form or another of society in its totality.

The debate over whether there are any laws of motion of industrial societies and, if so, what they are, has been going on for over a century and a half; the one clear conclusion is that there are ever more laws and ever more disagreement about them, and that there will be more of both. One useful way of looking at these laws and at the societies to which they supposedly relate is to compare and contrast the tendencies envisioned and those actually experienced for and against convergence among industrial societies. We turn next to tendencies experienced.

Evidence on Convergence
and Continuing Diversity

2

WHAT ARE the demonstrated economic performance capacities of different types of industrial societies? After disag-
gregating these societies into components, can we identify a
trend toward convergence in any of these separate components? For this latter purpose, the scheme of Marx is too
undifferentiated, dividing society into essentially only the
economic base structure, which is made up of the forces of
production (including technology) and the relations of production (including ownership of property), and the superstructure, which is made up of political institutions and patterns of belief and behavior. We need finer distinctions than
that to answer our questions in a meaningful way, and we
will therefore distinguish nine different aspects of society.

Nations can be divided into those organized basically along
private property and market economy lines, versus nations

organized more along public property and planned economy lines. The former are identified as "capitalist"; the latter are identified as "socialist," since each is operated under the authority of a communist party. They are, however, not communist in the sense used by Marx, but rather first-phase socialist societies. We will compare these two sets of countries, looking both at their totality and at variations within each set. Most of the data used will, of necessity, be for the United States, West Germany, France, the United Kingdom, and Japan, among what Benjamin Ward has called the "Affluent Fifteen,"[1] and for the USSR among the East European socialist nations, although it is in some important ways not typical of them. Our general field of concern will be the twenty-eight countries shown in Table 2.1. The statistical data, unfortunately, are less adequate than one might wish. The data given here are more indicative of conditions than conclusive about them. Ideally, comparable data should be used for all of the twenty-eight countries and over a substantial period of time; but they are not available.

It is misleading to concentrate too much on the United States and the USSR, as is often done, since they are often at the extremes; and much more similarity is shown if, for example, Sweden and the United Kingdom are compared and contrasted with Poland, Hungary, and Yugoslavia. Among the capitalist nations, Japan is distinctive in many ways but particularly because it is not yet, at least, a welfare-state capitalist society; among the socialist nations, Hungary and Yugoslavia are comparatively more oriented to the market. Also, some countries should be divided into component parts as though they were different nations. For example, per capita income variations are as much as two to one among regions of the USSR, and averages for the total nation are misleading about its component parts—the Baltic provinces are quite different from Central Asia.[2]

Convergence is concerned with the general direction of movement, rather than with current status alone. The central issue is not whether two or more situations are currently the same or not, but whether they are getting closer to each other over time, although, perhaps, still far apart. Movement may be faster or slower from time to time; convergence of East

Table 2.1. Statistical data for twenty-eight industrialized nations.

| Country | 1977 GNP per capita (exchange rates) | | 1977 GDP per capita (purchasing power parities) | | Percent of economically active population in agriculture, late 1970s (various years) |
	Rank	1977 U.S. dollars	Rank	1970 U.S. dollars	
Switzerland	1	11,080	12	3,664	16
Sweden	2	9,340	4	4,399	6
Denmark	3	9,160	8	4,219	9
United States	4	8,750	1	5,602	4
West Germany	5	8,620	3	4,434	6
Norway	6	8,570	6	4,385	11
Canada	7	8,350	2	4,949	5
Belgium	8	8,280	5	4,391	3
Netherlands	9	7,710	9	3,873	10
France	10	7,500	7	4,368	10
Australia	11	7,290	11	3,759	14
Japan	12	6,510	10	3,788	11
Austria	13	6,450	16	3,259	18
Finland	14	6,190	13	3,481	17
East Germany	15	5,070	—	—	9
United Kingdom	16	4,540	14	3,447	3
New Zealand	17	4,480	15	3,288	13
Czechoslovakia	18	4,240	—	—	14
Israel	19	3,760	17	3,088	6
Italy	20	3,530	18	2,719	15
USSR	21	3,330	—	—	24
Spain	23	3,260	19	2,411	19
Hungary	24	3,100	—	—	20
Ireland	25	3,060	20	2,388	25
Poland	22	3,290	—	—	32
Romania	26	3,000 (est.)	—	—	40
Bulgaria	27	2,830	—	—	27
Yugoslavia	28	2,100	—	—	32

Note: Industrialized nations are defined as those with a GNP per capita in 1977 of $3000 or more *and* 25 percent or less of the economically active population in agriculture. The last four nations do not meet this definition of industrialized societies but are included as being among the more advanced socialist economies. Not shown are nations whose high GNP per capita is based upon oil exports.

Table 2.1 (continued)

Sources: For GNP (gross national product): World Bank, *World Bank Atlas, 1979* (Washington, D.C.: World Bank, 1980). For GDP (gross domestic product): Robert Summers, Irving B. Kravis, and Alan Heston, "International Comparisons of Real Product and Its Composition: 1950–1977," *Review of Income and Wealth* 26 (March 1980): 19–66. For percent in agriculture: U.S. Central Intelligence Agency, *National Basic Intelligence Factbook* (Washington, D.C.: Government Printing Office, 1980).

and West, in comparative utilization of plans and markets, for example, was almost certainly faster in the 1950s than in the 1970s. At some point, movement may be blocked and may proceed no further. Reversals also are possible (as when Stalin reversed the New Economic Policy of Lenin in the 1920s, or when Mao introduced the Cultural Revolution in the 1960s); and even reversions to some earlier stage of history are possible, although this seems unlikely. Additionally, industrial societies may be entering a totally new stage of history with tighter resource constraints but new levels of knowledge. This, however, is pure speculation.

In exploring whether there has been a tendency toward convergence in the recent past and, more specifically, whether there has been a tendency for separate segments of industrial societies to become differentially more alike, we are dealing with a multidimensional problem.[3] Societies are not totally consistent, fully monolithic entities. They have their component parts, each of which is subject to differing varieties of constraints and pressures; and some parts must be looked at from more than a single point of view. For example, it is not enough to ask who owns what property; one must also ask who manages it and under what rules it is used. Thus, we shall be concerned here not only with different nations but also with separate segments of these societies and with their complexities. The central theme of this chapter is the multidimensional character of the internal life of social systems and the disjointed nature of their interior relations.

An analysis of experienced tendencies toward convergence and continuing diversity is central to an understanding of the historical course of industrial societies. Looking at such tendencies helps to show nations where they have been in recent times, where they are now, and where they seem to be headed in the near future in comparison with one another.

Survival and Performance Capacities of Systems of Industrialization

In *Industrialism and Industrial Man*, my colleagues and I set forth five main ways of organizing an industrial or industrializing society. We identified them by the elites that initially played the central role in the process: the middle class, as in eighteenth-century England; the dynastic families, as in nineteenth-century Germany; the colonial administrators, as in nineteenth-century India; the revolutionary intellectuals, as in twentieth-century Russia; and the nationalist leaders, as in twentieth-century Egypt. We noted, of course, that in practice there was a variety of combinations among these types that blurred clear-cut distinctions, particularly as each nation proceeded down the road to industrialism. Jan Szczepański, a leading Polish sociologist, has, among others, agreed with the importance attached to "the industrializing group," on the basis of the "political character of this group, its ideology and its aims" which "affect in a decisive way the economic model formed during the course of expansion."[4]

We went on to say that two of these systems — economies organized by dynastic elites and by colonial administrators — were transitory and had little future. The past twenty years of experience has been in accord with this conclusion. No nations continuing under these forms of organization have made the transition into advanced industrial societies. The dynastic elite approach in Iran, for example, has recently crumbled. Colonies have almost disappeared, although there are quasi-colonial relationships in, for example, former French West Africa.

Only systems with essential flaws, as in the colonial and the dynastic, were doomed to failure in recent times — the one doomed by the limitations of foreign domination, the other by the limitations of hereditary leadership. The former fell before the claims of nationalism; the latter has fallen or is falling before the claims of more egalitarian opportunities for meritocratic advancement into political leadership, and into managerial and professional ranks.

We thought, however, that the other three systems, in their

Table 2.2. Rates of growth of real national income per employed worker (in percent).

Country	1950–1967	1970–1977
Comecon countries	4	4
OECD countries	4	3
All lower-productivity countries	5	4

Sources: Figures for 1950–1967 from Abram Bergson, "Development under Two Systems: Comparative Productivity Growth since 1950," World Politics 23 (July 1971): 579–617; and idem, Productivity and the Social System: The USSR and the West (Cambridge, Mass.: Harvard University Press, 1978), p. 200. Figures for 1970–1977 calculated on the same basis.

many variations, all did have survival capacities, although we suggested that the last (the one organized by nationalist leaders) would move more in the middle-class direction in those nations where early efforts at industrialization were successful and more in the revolutionary-intellectual direction where they were not. To the extent that this view of the history of industrialization is approximately correct, a very great convergence has already taken place and is continuing to take place as major alternative methods of industrialization originally attempted (the dynastic and the colonial) have been eliminated or are being eliminated.

In the continuing and intensifying world-wide competition, capitalist economies and socialist economies have grown in recent times at somewhat the same rate, although the former slowed down comparatively in the 1970s in part because they were more affected by the oil crisis; the USSR has been self-sufficient in oil and has aided other socialist nations with oil supplies. As yet, neither type of system has buried the other, although this still remains a possibility for the future. The still industrializing nations (many under nationalist leaders) have generally been growing at somewhat higher rates. They start from a lower base, draw on accumulated technological knowledge, and sometimes also obtain capital resources from more developed societies (see Table 2.2). The survival capacity of these three types of systems runs contrary to the view of Marx a century ago which saw capitalism decaying rapidly into revolution, and of Hayek in more recent times who thought that only market systems could operate at all effectively. Although the socialist and capitalist types of systems have grown at about the same rate, they have done so from quite different base levels of output per employed worker (see Table 2.3). They may have played more or less "to a tie" in rates of growth, but not in levels of economic productivity.

Social welfare productivity, defined as the ability to support life and spread literacy, does not show any clear-cut advantage — as does economic productivity, for example — between capitalist and socialist types of societies. The so-called Physical Quality of Life Index (PQLI) has been devised to include the rate of infant mortality before age one, the level of life expectancy at age one, and the spread of literacy among adults.[5] A high rating on this index requires widespread educational opportunity, universally available health care facilities, and adequate levels of nutrition for the entire population. These, in turn, necessitate effective production and distribution of basic services and goods. Nations with relatively good records, given their general level of per capita income, are quite diverse in their essential economic and political orientations (Table 2.4). At the top of the entire list are Western market economies: Sweden in the lead, followed by Denmark, Iceland, Japan, the Netherlands, and Norway. Romania and Bulgaria have done comparatively well among the socialist nations, which, overall, have higher indices than

Table 2.3. Real national income per employed worker (U.S. = 100).

Country	1960	1977
Comecon countries	27	34
OECD countries	47	76

Sources: Figures for 1960 from Abram Bergson, "Development under Two Systems: Comparative Productivity Growth since 1950," World Politics 23 (July 1971): 579-617; and idem, Productivity in the Social System: The USSR and the West (Cambridge, Mass.: Harvard University Press, 1978), p. 200. Figures for 1977 calculated on the same basis.

Table 2.4. Physical Quality of Life Index (PQLI) for selected countries grouped by average per capita GNP, early 1970s. (Listed in ascending order of per capita GNP within each group.)

GNP category	PQLI[a]	Number of countries
A. *Per capita GNP under $500*		25
Kampuchea	40	
Laos	31	
Bangladesh	35	
Nepal	25	
Burma	51	
India	43	
Afghanistan	18	
Pakistan	38	
Haiti	36	
Sri Lanka	82	
Yemen Arab Republic	27	
Vietnam	54	
Indonesia	48	
Yemen, People's Republic	33	
China, People's Republic[b]	69	
Western Samoa	84	
Thailand	68	
Bolivia	43	
Philippines	71	
Honduras	51	
El Salvador	64	
Jordan	47	
Papua New Guinea	37	
South Korea	82	
Grenada	77	
Mean:	50	
B. *Per capita GNP $500–$1,000*		19
Ecuador	68	
Colombia	71	
Albania[b]	75	
Paraguay	75	

Table 2.4 (continued)

GNP category	PQLI[a]	Number of countries
Guatemala	54	
Guyana	85	
Dominican Republic	64	
Cuba[b]	84	
Nicaragua	54	
Syria	54	
Malaysia	66	
Peru	62	
Turkey	55	
Lebanon	79	
Taiwan	86	
Costa Rica	85	
Brazil	68	
Fiji	80	
Mexico	73	
Mean:	70	
C. *Per capita GNP $1,000–$2,000*		18
Jamaica	84	
Malta	87	
Romania[b]	90	
Chile	77	
Panama	80	
Guadeloupe	76	
Uruguay	87	
Surinam	83	
Argentina	85	
Yugoslavia[b]	84	
Barbados	89	
Cyprus	85	
Portugal	80	
Martinique	83	
Hong Kong	86	
Netherlands Antilles	82	
Bulgaria[b]	91	
Trinidad and Tobago	85	

Table 2.4 (continued)

GNP category	PQLI[a]	Number of countries
	Mean: 84	
D. *Per capita GNP $2,000–$3,000*		10
Singapore	83	
Greece	89	
Venezuela	79	
Hungary[b]	91	
Puerto Rico	90	
Ireland	93	
USSR[b]	91	
Spain	91	
Poland[b]	91	
Italy	92	
	Mean: 89	
E. *Per capita GNP $3,000–$4,000*		5
Bahamas	84	
Czechoslovakia[b]	93	
Israel	89	
United Kingdom	94	
East Germany[b]	93	
	Mean: 91	
F. *Per capita GNP over $4,000*		17
Japan	96	
New Zealand	94	
Austria	93	
Finland	94	
Australia	93	
Netherlands	96	
France	94	
Iceland	96	
Belgium	93	
Luxembourg	92	
Norway	96	
West Germany	93	
Canada	95	

Table 2.4 (continued)

GNP category	PQLI[a]	Number of countries
Denmark	96	
United States	94	
Sweden	97	
Switzerland	95	
	Mean: 95	

a. The Physical Quality of Life Index is made up of three components: infant mortality rates, life expectancy at age one, and literacy. The first two are based on a "best" and "worst" case system of indexing, using historical data from 1950 to the early 1970s. The literacy component is the literacy rate as percent of population. The three measures are indexed on a scale of zero to one hundred and are then averaged to obtain the PQLI.

b. Under socialist system for a significant period of time before the early 1970s.

Source: Prepared from Morris David Morris, *Measuring the Condition of the World's Poor: The Physical Quality of Life Index* (New York: Pergamon Press, for the Overseas Development Council, 1979), app. B, table 1.

Note: This list omits African nations and Middle East oil countries.

the average of the per capita income groups within which they fall. Geographic location is a major explanation of ratings, with African nations (except South Africa) ranking generally very low and oil-exporting nations of the Middle East ranking very low in comparison with the levels of their per capita GNP (gross national product). Both sets of nations have been omitted from Table 2.4. European and North American nations rank quite high, as do those in Oceania. Generally, the level of per capita GNP and geographic location are more explanatory of the PQLI than is the nature of the social system; although, as noted, socialist nations (given their GNP levels per capita and taking into account also their geographic locations) do relatively well.

The conditions of past decades have made it relatively easy for a variety of economic systems to survive and to be at least minimally effective. There has generally been a sufficiency of natural resources, a rapidly developing technology, and a consensus in all nations on the desirability of economic growth. The tests of the next several decades may be more difficult ones. During the past century, however, it has been possible for several types of systems to keep on bringing year-to-year improvements in living standards for their people and social peace for their societies. This may not be so in the next century. The hard tests may lie ahead.

Segments of Industrial Societies

1. *The content of knowledge.* "Technical knowledge . . . is the common property of the epoch; it is international in character."[6] So also is science, as well as music and literature. Access may be limited in some nations to a small elite, but in any advanced industrial society, professionals have world-wide knowledge within their specialties. The exception, and usually a short-lived one, is secretly held science and technology.

"Knowledge," Alfred Marshall wrote, "is our most powerful engine of production."[7] The modern age began with the realization that "knowledge is power," to use the words of Francis Bacon. Industrialization itself began with new knowledge about steam and machinery. This is where the "great transformation" began.

We see, in particular, substantial agreement among scientists on what constitutes the truth — they form the first really international community. We see rising interest among scientists of many nations in the environmental concerns and the global perspectives that Harrison Brown, among others, has raised.[8] And the high culture, consisting of the intellectual and artistic content of knowledge, becomes more alike throughout advanced industrial societies. Some of the same books are read, some of the same musical compositions are listened to, and some of the same forms of art are viewed. Daniel Bell prefers to identify this as "internationalization" rather than as an aspect of convergence,[9] reserving the term "convergence" for developments particularly in political structures.

Limitations on access to high culture are more likely to be placed on the intelligentsia in socialist than in capitalist nations, but these limitations are always subject to attack and to erosion. The clear trend has been for science and high culture to become more universal. The instruments of industrial society make this possible; the interests and tastes of highly educated people everywhere make it likely. Knowledge knows no national boundaries.

2. *The mobilization of the resources of production.* "Production," Marx wrote, "appears as the starting point."[10] Each industrial nation, regardless of type, has tried to mobilize its resources of production in an effective way. These resources of production have everywhere been the same, although there have been variations in the extent of their availability and in the way they are assembled. These variations in assembly, however, have been in degree, not in kind.

Each nation has sought to utilize the best modern technology. This has been a particularly intense effort where there is a military confrontation (as between the United States and Russia) or where industries are in international competition with each other (as in automobiles and electronics). But it has also been true in more domestic pursuits such as medical care and food production, where international comparisons are relatively easily made and where domestic demand is intense.

The USSR is generally slower than the United States to adopt new techniques. Estimates of the lag vary from three years[11] to five to ten years, although the USSR and the East are ahead of the United States and the West in some areas.[12] These lags are not of great consequence in the long run, but they may be very important even in the very short run in the military arena. There are lags not only in the first adoption of new techniques but also in their diffusion throughout a nation; and it is costly in foreign exchange to purchase techniques abroad and psychologically debilitating to have to do so, both for the leaders of the nation and for its scientists and technologists.

Each nation has increased its percentage of the GNP spent on research and development (R&D), although leadership nations within each type have tended to be the most aggressive in this regard. Some nations, however, have historically relied more on R&D efforts of other nations. Japan once did, but by the early 1970s it seemed to have caught up with U.S.

levels of technology through its own efforts in applied R&D.[13] One definition of industrial leadership, and one indication of changing leadership among nations, is the percentage of GNP spent on R&D; according to this measure, both Germany and Japan have been catching up with the United States. Generally, each nation has greatly elevated its emphasis upon the production, accumulation, and utilization of new scientific and technological knowledge. The overall figure for capitalist societies for investment in R&D is now around 2 percent of GNP for the most advanced nations, with the USSR at 4 percent. But even so, the USSR still tends to lag in most areas in the introduction of new technology, although this heavy emphasis on R&D has certainly helped it catch up with the United States from an estimated lag of twenty-five years (within a range of five to forty years in different fields) in 1962.[14] The East European socialist nations stand at about 2 percent. (The appendix gives some of the relevant statistics on this and on other subjects that follow. For a summary, see Table 2.5.)

Each nation has sought to find and to exploit its own raw materials or, where necessary, to assemble them from around the earth.

Each nation has greatly increased its expenditure of energy per capita. The past century of great world-wide economic development has been based increasingly on energy from oil. It has been the age of oil; and not just modern capitalism but also socialism has been built upon it.

Each nation has sought to mobilize capital investment, and capital investment has grown historically as a percentage of the gross domestic product (GDP). It now stands generally at 20 to 35 percent in industrialized nations. Bergson calculated gross fixed investment as a percent of GNP, from 1950 to 1966, as 25 percent for the Comecon countries (members of the Council for Mutual Economic Assistance) and 21 percent for the OECD countries (members of the Organization for Economic Cooperation and Development). More recent figures (1966–1978) show a continuation of these variations but at a somewhat higher level of 29 versus 23 percent (partly because of a shift in calculations from a GNP to a national in-

Table 2.5. Areas of comparability, increasing similarity, and continuing substantial dissimilarity between capitalist and socialist nations today.

Current comparability	Increasing similarity	Continuing substantial dissimilarity
Rates of economic growth	Percent of population in agriculture	Level of income per employed worker
Social welfare productivity in terms of life expectancy and levels of literacy	Percent of adult women in labor force	Percent of GNP expended for investment
Utilization of technology	Percent of labor force in service and white-collar occupations	Percent of students in higher education enrolled in science, engineering, and agriculture
Elevated expenditures on R&D	Percent of population in large urban areas	Time spent standing in lines at shops
Expenditures on health and education	Percent of labor force self-employed	Comparative rate of pay for white-collar workers
Utilization of large-scale manufacturing enterprises	Ability of managers to dismiss workers	Percent of national income spent on current consumption
Existence of substantial numbers of professionals and technicians in labor force	Content of work rules	Amount of acknowledged inflation
Increased occupational and geographic mobility	Distribution of income	Amount of open unemployment
Creation of a "web of rules" governing the workplace	Use of property	Ownership of property
Hours of work per week		Use of plans and markets
Length of working life		Autonomy of organizations of workers (except for Yugoslavia among the socialist nations)
Use of nonworking time		Distribution of ultimate political power
Net reproduction rate		Religious beliefs, national and ethnic identities, and personality traits and behavior
Wage differentials for skill		Goals of economic and political systems
Prestige scores for occupations		
Interindustry wage differentials		
Welfare expenditures as percent of GNP		
Government expenditures as percent of GNP		

come or GDP basis). Japan is high among the OECD countries, and the United States and United Kingdom are low (see Table 2.6).

Each nation has sought to mobilize its labor force for industrial production. This has meant drawing workers out of agriculture and putting women into the employed labor force. Nonagricultural employment in the industrialized nations now stands at or above about 90 percent of total employment, with the USSR at nearly 80 percent (see Table 2 of the appendix). The percentage of adult women in the labor force stands at 30 to 40 percent, with the USSR at 46 percent. In Italy, where traditional views regarding the mother's place in the home are widely held, the figure is a low 25 percent, and it is much lower than that in Muslim countries — 5 percent — where for religious reasons women's activities are limited.[15]

Mobilizing the labor force has meant encouraging better health, and one common index of modernization has been the number of medical doctors, nurses, paramedical personnel, and dentists per hundred thousand people. It has also meant more emphasis upon education — on universal literacy, on the training of technicians, on the creation of more engineers and scientists and managers. It has spurred attempts to recruit high-level talent from within all classes of society. Better edu-

Table 2.6. Capital investment as a percentage of national income.

Country	1950–1966 (in percent)	1966–1978 (in percent)
Comecon countries	25[a]	29[b]
OECD countries	21[a]	23[c]

a. Of GNP.
b. Of national income.
c. Of GDP.
Sources: Figures for 1950–1966 from Abram Bergson, "Development under Two Systems," World Politics 23 (July 1971): 579–617. Figures for 1966–1978 calculated from OECD, Quarterly National Accounts Bulletin, 1979, vol. 4 (Paris: OECD, 1979); and from Comecon, Statistical Yearbook (Moscow: Comecon, 1979; English language edition London: IPC Industrial Press, 1979), table 18.

cational systems have led to substantial contributions to output. Japan, among the capitalist nations, has been preeminent in maximizing capital investment and investment in human capital combined; the United Kingdom has lagged. The United States has a very high rate of enrollments in tertiary education partially due to open-access enrollment in many of its institutions; and the USSR has a high ratio of tertiary enrollments in agriculture, science, and engineering programs as a matter of developmental policy (see Table 3 of the appendix).

The emphases in mobilization of the resources of production have varied somewhat from nation to nation and by type of society. The socialist nations have put more stress on capital accumulation, on R&D (in the case of the USSR), and on investment in human capital. However, their real output per person has generally been substantially lower than under capitalism, which implies that their efficiency in using physical and human capital has been much lower; inputs have been comparatively higher than outputs, efforts have been comparatively greater than results. They have been more aggressive in mobilizing their productive resources but less efficient in their utilization, particularly in the use of managers and the use of workers. But then, it should be noted that they are generally at an earlier stage of economic development (see Table 4 of the appendix).

An important distinction must be made between productivity and efficiency.[16] The socialist countries are less productive in output per worker partly because they are less efficient, but also because they have, in some respects, poorer resources (agricultural land in the USSR, for example, is of lesser quality than that in the United States) and they have less up-to-date technology. The lower efficiency is due to many factors, including the inadequacies of central planning that result in constant stoppages for lack of raw materials and parts, the handicaps on effective use of workers inherent in enforced individual job security, and the distortions caused by price controls. Price controls put an emphasis on quantity versus quality; often result in a surplus of money over goods and services that causes long lines at shops and a reduced incentive to work; lead to distortions in the use of resources; and encourage the creation of special supply sources for the elites and other forms of corruption (among other negative effects). Also, agricultural policy has been a dismal failure in most of the socialist countries—another explanation for inefficiency.

There are great variations in efficiency not only between capitalist and socialist nations but also among capitalist nations—as, for example, between Japan and the United Kingdom. The determinants of this comparative efficiency are highly varied and deserve much more intensive examination than they have had. Harvey Leibenstein has written of "X-efficiency" and "X-inefficiency."[17]

Factors involved include the degree of inertia in the system, the quality of the management, and the degree of effort put forth by the human participants. These vary greatly. Generally, it would seem that state enterprise is under less pressure to reduce inertia, improve management and mobilize human energy than is private enterprise, whether within socialist or capitalist systems, and is subject to more constraints.

There are great differences among the United Kingdom, Japan, the United States, and the USSR. The United Kingdom has a low rate of capital investment and output per worker. The United States has a low rate of capital investment but a high rate of output per worker. Japan is higher than the United Kingdom in both respects but lower than the United States in output per worker. The USSR has a high rate of capital investment but a very low rate of output per worker (see Table 2.7).

Generally it may be said, nevertheless, that industrial societies despite their dissimilarities have gone about the mobilization of the same types of resources of production and in somewhat similar ways.

3. *The organization of production.* Here again there are some similarities. The industrial nations all create manufacturing, construction, and transportation industries. They all build service industries to aid the industrial segment and to support the population; and the distribution of effort between industry and service becomes much alike—roughly in

Table 2.7. Output per worker and capital investment.

Country	Output per employed person, 1977 (in U.S. dollars)	Gross domestic investment as percent of GDP, 1978
United States	21,000	16
Japan	14,000	31
United Kingdom	10,000	18
USSR	7,000	31

Sources: Output per employed person: calculated from GNP at market prices from World Bank, *World Bank Atlas, 1979* (Washington, D.C.: World Bank, 1980); and OECD, *Labour Force Statistics, 1967–1978* (Paris: OECD, 1980). Investment figures for the United States, the United Kingdom, and Japan: OECD, *Quarterly National Accounts Bulletin, 1979*, vol. 4 (Paris: OECD, 1979). Investment figures for the USSR: Herbert Block, "Soviet Economic Performance in a Global Context," in *Soviet Economy in a Time of Change*, vol. 1, Joint Economic Committee, 96th Congress, 1st sess. (Washington, D.C.: Government Printing Office, 1979), p. 137.

the proportion of forty to sixty (see Tables 1 and 5 of the appendix).

There are differences, however. The USSR has concentrated comparatively more effort on heavy industry than have the capitalist nations. The distribution in the USSR between industry and service is now more like fifty to fifty than the more usual forty to sixty (it was sixty to forty in the USSR as recently as in the 1960s). The heavy emphasis on military hardware (defense activities absorb somewhere around 12 percent of the GNP) is one explanation (see Table 6 of the appendix).[18] The "ideological bias against so-called nonproductive activities" is another.[19] But this ratio has been changing as the economy becomes more advanced, as more communal services must be created to keep women in the labor force, and as ideology is less rigidly followed; and the USSR may be going a "good part of the way towards a normal pattern."[20]

The occupational structure in the USSR reflects this comparatively heavy emphasis on manufacturing, construction, and transportation. In contrast to capitalist nations, fewer people are employed in tertiary segment occupations, particularly in clerical work and in sales, although this is not true of professional and technical positions.[21] More are employed as engineers and as railway workers.[22] The USSR also has relatively more teachers and fewer enterprise managers. The smaller numbers of clerical workers (and the meager responsibilities given to them) means that clerical tasks are pushed upward on professional and technical personnel and on managers and often are not well done, as many Westerners have observed in the USSR. The smaller numbers of sales personnel mean lines in shops and poor service. The smaller numbers of people classified as managers may be misleading because there is a tendency to classify people actually in managerial positions as engineers or professionals or technicians. Managerial responsibilities are also pushed up the line.

The new production activities are concentrated in urban areas. Most manufacturing employees are located in enterprises of substantial size (see Table 5 of the appendix).

Much less work everywhere gets performed within the family. Most members of the labor force are employees. The number of self-employed goes down drastically, although Japan still has an unusually high number of self-employed persons in agriculture and in the crafts. Many managers everywhere are themselves employees. Fewer of the managers in any system are also owners. The authority split in society is less between the workers and the capitalists, as Marx saw it, and more between the many grades of the managed and the many grades of the managers. The class of managers becomes comparatively larger and very fractionated by task and by level of authority. A new class of professionals and technicians is also created.

The labor force decreasingly has within it people with largely inherited status, such as farmers. It tends to become divided between people whose careers are ruled by seniority and those ruled by competitive merit, such as athletes and musicians; the former tend to become dominant in numbers and to grow in comparative importance. Stratification by inheritance gives way to stratification by merit, and particularly to stratification by seniority.

As the division of labor becomes more intensified, as the

number of occupations and suboccupations grows, people come to think of themselves in terms of many more categories than simply peasant or landlord, worker or owner. They have many occupational identifications.

A mobility system becomes essential. People must be distributed among many occupations and several geographic areas. And as Seymour Martin Lipset has noted, mobility rates are "comparable in socialist and capitalist countries" and mobility faces much the same "major barriers" in each type of system.[23] The Soviet Union also has "strata," much as in the West, with "systematic differences in incomes and living standards, in control over the organization of the work place, in the educational and occupational opportunities open to their children."[24] The educational system, nevertheless, becomes a great sorting mechanism. So also does the labor market.

4. *Patterns of work.* Convergence in the mobilization of the resources of production and in the organization of production has had a clear impact on patterns of working life across nations and across systems.

Since the managed, the managers, and the professionals and technicians all work within larger and larger employing units, personal relations tend to become more formal. The employing unit becomes more bureaucratized in its operations.

The use of work time is subject to strict control. Lewis Mumford once remarked that "the clock, not the steam engine, is the key machine of the industrial age."[25]

The "web of rules" that Abraham Siegel and I once set forth[26] governs weekly hours of work (which now cluster around forty), the amount and timing of vacations, the hiring, firing, and promotion of workers, the handling of grievances, the amount of work to be performed, and much more. These rules, with some exceptions, are much alike from nation to nation, from sector to sector, and from industry to industry. The great exception is in the restricted ability of managers in socialist societies to dismiss employees, but there has also been some reduction in this ability in capitalist nations. Generally these "chains" of rules are stronger and more tightly fastened in socialist than in capitalist nations. Neither workers nor managers in either type of system, however, ever lose their "chains" in the form of the many rules that come to govern them all. The very interdependence of one production process with another, of one service with another, means that each participant must behave in a predictable way at a predictable time, and thus in accordance with set rules of conduct.

Engels once said that over the entrance of every factory should be written, "Leave, ye that enter here, all autonomy behind!" He also wrote, "If man, by dint of his knowledge and inventive genius, has subdued the forces of nature, the latter avenge themselves upon him by subjecting him, in so far as he employs them, to a veritable despotism independent of all social organisation. Wanting to abolish authority in large-scale industry is tantamount to wanting to abolish industry itself, to destroy the power loom in order to return to the spinning wheel."[27]

It should be noted that different industries have their own cultures—the work cultures of the farmers, the seamen, the construction workers, the coal miners, the assembly line workers, the bank clerks. These cultures are much alike among nations. There is a much greater difference among industrial working cultures within a nation than there is within the same industrial culture among nations. There are more similarities in the working lives of coal miners in Russia and in the United States than between coal miners and bank clerks in either of these nations. Occupation is more important to the nature of the individual working life than is the national economic and political structure. A person's working life on the job is more defined by saying "I am a coal miner" than by saying "I am a Pole" or "I am German."[28]

There are, however, differences. In socialist systems the mobility system is more responsive to determination by the state and less to the desires of individuals, the web of rules more complete and confining, and open unemployment very substantially reduced. The overwhelming fact, however, is that in patterns of work life the jobs and the rules governing work are mostly similar from nation to nation and from one type of society to the other. And in the workplace there now seem to be some nearly universal trends toward more emphasis on seniority on the job, more participation in work-place decisions, and more options in such arrangements as work time and the use of fringe benefits.

5. *Patterns of living.* Patterns of daily living, outside of work, also tend to converge. Lifetime use of years, in education, in employment, in retirement, becomes more alike. John D. Durand found, in a study of one hundred countries, a tendency to enter the labor force later and to leave it earlier, with a convergence on age twenty to enter and sixty-five to leave.[29] Years of life expectancy tend to become more comparable (see Table 5 of the appendix).

Daily and weekly use of time also becomes much the same — time spent in traveling to work, in listening to the radio and viewing television, and in many other ways. One substantial exception is time spent standing in lines, which is much greater in socialist nations with planned economies, reflecting their lesser efficiency and their lesser attention to consumer markets.[30] Another is less time spent on religious observances in these same societies (except Poland).

Alexander Szalai of Hungary made a study of the use of time in twelve countries, half of them capitalist and half socialist. He was "profoundly impressed at the many similarities in time expenditure that are registered in the everyday lives of people interviewed across twelve quite various societies," and concluded that these "striking similarities . . . can readily be attributed to the common imprint of industrialization." He noted that "there is no continental divide running through Europe and separating human aspirations and cultural behavior in the West and in the East." He particularly sympathized with the universal "plight of the employed woman who has to act also as a housekeeper to her family" under both socialism and capitalism.[31] Overall, the differences in patterns of daily life are surprisingly small, considering the big differences in the standards of living, in the social systems, and in traditional cultural patterns.

In industrial nations, most people come to reside in urban areas; to live in nuclear rather than extended families; to have fewer children — with the net reproduction rate approaching or falling below the replacement rate; to spend proportionately less of their income on food; to have fewer persons living in each room; to make more use of electronic equipment — telephone, radio, television; to obtain more durable goods, particularly automobiles; to travel more; to spend more of their incomes on their health. Their lives are spent less in contact with nature, more in contact with man-made products and environments — and these products and environments are much alike from nation to nation (see Table 7 of the appendix).

Everywhere all of life, not just life in the workplace, has become more subject to bureaucratic rules.

Lifestyles, particularly among educated youth and the professional classes, tend to become more cosmopolitan, and there is more similarity in the clothes people wear, the food they eat, and the music to which they listen. There comes to be an international, up-to-date style of life — what Soedjatmoko has called the new "cosmopolitan culture."[32]

An industrial pattern of daily life is thus created. The daily lives of people in industrial nations are more homogenized than ever was the situation in earlier forms of civilization. To find any great variety, one must now look at preindustrial societies.

Regarding the prospective transition from capitalism into socialism, Schumpeter wrote that "there is the world of the laborer and the clerk. No reform of souls, no painful adaptation would be required of them. Their work would remain substantially what it is — and would . . . turn out similar attitudes and habits. From his work the laborer or the clerk would return to a home and to pursuits . . . which would still be the same kind of home and the same kind of pursuits."[33] And Marion J. Levy, Jr., observed that "more and more of what all peoples do will be explicable in terms of the phenomena of modernization."[34]

Industrialism leads to convergence in patterns of living *among* nations but to diversification *within* nations due to all the new types of life situations it opens up.

6. *Patterns of distribution of economic rewards.* As industrialism proceeds, economic rewards come to be based more on merit and on seniority and less on inherited status or on political acceptability, and the distribution of income after

taxes becomes more equal within individual nations, after having become less equal during earlier periods of industrialization.[35] Generally, the trend toward equalization has been more pronounced within socialist than within capitalist nations, but the distributions within Sweden and the United Kingdom and the USSR are much the same. Most people come to live within a distribution range of disposable income of two or two and a half to one. Capitalist nations tend to vary from socialist ones more in the spread at the extremes, between the top 5 and bottom 5 percent, than among the bulk of the people in the middle half of the income range where the difference is less than two to one in the socialist, and less than two and a half to one in the capitalist nations as based on the ratio of the seventy-fifth percentile to the twenty-fifth percentile (see Tables 8 and 9 of the appendix). The major difference in origin of income between the two systems is due to income from property, which amounts to about 25 percent of national income in Western nations.[36] But in general, "the differences in the distribution of income between the planned socialist economies and the capitalist welfare states are relatively minor."[37] The apparent differences would probably be narrowed even more if the "second economy," corruption, and the preferred status of elites as consumers in the socialist nations could be taken into account.

Wage differentials among manual workers, in terms of premiums for high skills, generally drop from 200–400 percent in industrializing countries to 25–50 percent in advanced countries.[38] South Africa is a great exception, where differentials of ten to one and more were maintained in the gold-mining industry for over half a century as a result of apartheid, although they are being reduced somewhat now. In his classic study of wage differentials, Henry Phelps Brown found that the grades of work requiring more education, experience, and skill, and carrying more responsibility, have been universally more highly paid. This has been found to be so even in Mao's China and Castro's Cuba. It shows that "the inequality of pay arises from factors common to societies of very various economic, political and social complexions." The one major exception is that "in the Soviet-type economies the lower administrative, technical and clerical workers are paid less than many manual workers." But "the white-collared apart, the most remarkable feature of the comparison between the Soviet-type and Western-type wage structures is the extent of their similarity."[39] The comparatively low pay for white-collar workers in Soviet-type societies is due, in part, to ideological considerations but also to the pressure of more women in the labor force and the heavy investment in the education of workers. Each type of society must respond to labor market forces. Even a socialist economy has limits on its ability "to impose whatever reward structure it pleases"; and "Soviet socialist ideology has more in common with . . . meritocratic views . . . than with . . . egalitarianism."[40]

Interindustry wage differentials relate to skill differentials and thus they, too, narrow. Metal working everywhere remains high and textiles low, reflecting their differing skill levels (see Table 10 of the appendix).[41]

The prestige accorded to different occupations is also quite similar. In a study covering six countries (the USSR, Japan, the United Kingdom, New Zealand, the United States, and Germany), medical doctors always ranked high and unskilled workers low and, overall, there was a "marked degree of agreement" on prestige levels. There were some variations: engineers, for example, ranked unusually high in the USSR, and farmers ranked high in the United States.[42] However, since this study was made, there may have been a decline in the status of engineers, paralleling a fall in their pay differentials (see Table 6 of the appendix).[43]

Compensation becomes more highly structured, less of an individual matter, and skill and seniority differentials more rigidly fixed. Fringe benefits for health and retirement become a larger part of compensation. These are universal tendencies.

Compared with earlier times, more of the income in all nations today is subject to redistribution by government by way of welfare and social insurance programs. The general range of welfare state expenditures is 15 to 25 percent of gross national production, actually somewhat higher on the average in capitalist than in socialist nations (although Japan is the lowest), but then the former have substantially higher rates of open unemployment, define more potential members of the labor force as unemployable, and have, thus far at least, more retired workers (see Table 11 of the appendix). Harold Wilensky, in his study entitled *Welfare State and Equality*, found a convergence in welfare state expenditures with rising wealth regardless of the economic or political system.[44]

Total consumption expenditures as a percentage of GNP are much the same among the capitalist nations but somewhat lower in the socialist societies, where the state is more successful in capturing income for industrial and military investment purposes (see Table 6 of the appendix).

Inflation in capitalist nations is substantial. It is generally modest in amount in planned socialist nations, according to official accounts (0 to 2 percent a year in the 1960s and early 1970s), but certainly it is greater if the "second economy" outside the plan is taken into account. And unemployment officially does not exist in these nations (although there is "frictional" unemployment of perhaps 2 to 3 percent, and much unemployment or underemployment on the job), but it does exist to significant degree in capitalist nations. There is, however, clearly some underemployment in socialist economies, and a heavy price in efficiency is paid for the lack of ability of managers to dismiss workers. However, "according to conventional measures, such as inflation rates and unemployment, the planned socialist economies appear to be more stable than their capitalist counterparts."[45]

7. *The economic structure.* All mobilization of productive resources takes place within an economic structure. This structure includes the ownership of property, the management of enterprises, the goals of management, the rules governing management, the environments of management, and the competitors for managerial authority.

Marx overemphasized the importance of the ownership of property in the conduct of a society. He saw the possibility of only two economic structures, one based on private property and one based on public property. He totally neglected the independent role of political power as against economic power, which he thought solely determined political power; the two were coterminous. He also ignored the influence of individuals as consumers and as workers, whether organized or unorganized. He did see the beginning of the separation between ownership and management in capitalist societies — "the capitalist disappears as superfluous from the production process";[46] he did not, however, recognize how this might affect the operations of a capitalist (or socialist) society, with the managers becoming a force in their own right and not just hired overseers of the same continuing level of exploitation of workers. Most industrial property is now managed by professional managers whether the property is owned privately or publicly. The contrast in behavior is not as stark between professional managers of private property and professional managers of public property as Marx thought it was between private owners, who acted only in their own interests, and public owners, who acted only in the interests of the people.

Yet there are major differences. The private system is more oriented toward the consumer market and toward making a profit, and is more decentralized in decision making. The public system is more oriented toward fulfilling the plan and toward ensuring survival of the managers by meeting the requirements of the plan, and is more centralized in decision making.

On the other hand, there are some increasing similarities. Public controls over the use of property and centralized planning or guidance increase in the private systems; and market tests are more applied in the public systems, as in Hungary and Yugoslavia — and even in the USSR, as the "second economy" grows outside the plan. Both systems witness the rise of a technostructure of professionals and technicians that influences the top leaders but does not control them. Both systems develop pluralistic systems of industrial relations at the shop level in which technical rule making is shared by the state, the enterprise managers, and representatives of the workers. But there is the major difference that the participants on behalf of the workers are substantially autonomous in the private system but not in the public one; in the former, they have the right to organize self-governing associations, the right to strike, and the right to engage in political activity.[47] Both systems are subject to swings in the volume of economic activity — several of the systems in

Eastern Europe were in the early 1980s in a depression, although the swings are possibly both greater and certainly more obvious in the private systems (see Table 12 of the appendix). Both systems rely heavily on forced savings to accumulate capital — "forced" in the sense that savings are not made by individuals acting directly in their own behalf.

The overall situation today might broadly be described as follows.

Ownership of property in capitalist societies is more private than public, but there is much public property; in socialist societies ownership is more public than private, but some public property is treated as private — one-quarter to one-third of all agricultural production (other than grains) in both the USSR and China is from private plots. One-fifth of all livestock in the USSR is privately owned, and half of the housing space is personally owned. And a higher percentage of the labor force works in nationally owned enterprises in Austria than in Yugoslavia (see Table 13 of the appendix).

Regulation of the use of property is more private than public in capitalist societies, but Schumpeter could write of the prospective transition of capitalism to "socialism," by which he meant publicly controlled capitalism, essentially with reference to increasing regulation and not to transfer of ownership. In socialist societies there is more public regulation of property than private.

Separation of ownership and management is substantial in both systems.

In both systems there has been significant development of a level of professionals and technicians with some independent influence, but their independent impact is greater under capitalism.

Both systems use both markets and plans, with much greater emphasis on markets in capitalism and on plans in socialism; but there has been a tendency for more reliance on some form of macro, or even micro, planning (or at least guidance) in capitalism, and on markets in socialism. There is, of course, a very big difference between meeting the desires of the consumers and making a profit, and meeting the terms of the plan and surviving.

In both systems there has been extensive development of

organizations of workers and of rules governing the work-place based on tripartite discussions, but such organizations and rules are based on autonomous authority only in capital-ism. John T. Dunlop, in his book *Industrial Relations Systems*, presents the classic discussion of the similarities and differences among them. All "industrial societies necessarily create industrial relations, defined as the complex of inter-rela-tions among managers, workers and agencies of government." And "every industrial relations system creates a complex of rules to govern the work place and work community."[48]

No capitalist systems are any longer pure laissez-faire capitalism, and no socialist systems are pure state socialism (with the possible exception of Albania). Most are mixtures; but the capitalist mixtures are still far apart from the socialist mixtures. The greatest mixture is Yugoslavia which may be said to be one-third socialist, one-third capitalist, and one-third syndicalist. Capitalism may have become "creeping socialism" and socialism may have become "creeping capitalism," but they still stand far apart in methods and in results. The key differences between the two systems are, I believe, their respective degrees of reliance on the market and the plan, and their respective degrees of independence for organizations of workers. The first was a key issue in the "Prague Spring" of 1968. The second has been the key issue in Poland since August 1980.

8. *The political structure.* The political structure includes methods of selecting state leaders, mechanisms for develop-ing public policy, means for administering the state ap-paratus, and the system of law. All industrial nations develop a substantial state apparatus—the state does not "wither away" under socialism except in the very special sense of the demise of the capitalist-controlled state, which Marx viewed as an instrument for suppression of the workers. In fact, the role of government nearly everywhere increases with economic development. Adjusted state budget expenditures generally range from around 25 to 35 percent of gross na-tional production in both capitalist and socialist nations (see Tables 6 and 14 of the appendix). Frederic L. Pryor concludes his careful study *Public Expenditures in Communist and*

Capitalist Nations by saying that "in regard to public consumption expenditures there are few essential differences between nations of the two systems." The "policy dilemmas" are quite similar and the "decisions taken are also roughly similar." One main difference among the fourteen nations he studied was the high expenditure for military purposes by the two superpowers, the USSR and the United States.[49]

All industrial societies have their own national sovereignty; none is a colony. All industrial states work hard to achieve a consensus on how society should be organized, to persuade their citizens of the superiority or at least acceptability of their system. Whether through persuasion or control, there is a clear tendency for political violence to decline in the course of economic development. Where the systems differ most is in whether they have a monopoly of power in a single party (socialist states) or a competitive party system (capitalist states), and this is an enormous difference.

There does seem to be some tendency toward greater diffusion of political influence as nations become more affluent, have a more educated populace, and are more modernized; but this is somewhat deceptive, since most of the more affluent states are capitalist (see Tables 15 and 16 of the appendix). Irma Adelman and Cynthia Taft Morris have made the most careful studies of the relationship of social and political variables to economic advancement. They found a general tendency for increased social and political participation but concluded that "perhaps the principal lesson suggested by the above results is that increases in political participation are by no means automatic consequences of socioeconomic development."[50] There is no indication that greater affluence has led to competitive party systems in the socialist states.

Advanced capitalist states, of course, can and have turned fascist, as Germany did in the 1930s. There is no guarantee that, under severe pressure, they will always maintain a competitive party system. And a new kind of state socialism with competitive parties is certainly conceivable, although it has never yet developed. But it is certainly easier for the economic structure of a socialist state to move toward competition in the market than for the political structure to move toward competition among independent parties.

The political structure, it seems, does not always follow the economic structure. There is no assurance that capitalism guarantees democracy or that socialism guarantees dictatorship, no inevitability that capitalism degenerates into fascism or that socialism evolves into democracy. National history, historical accidents, and geographic location seem to play a more major role in determining the political structure than does the economic structure. There is no necessary one-to-one relationship between economic structure and political structure, although private enterprise in the marketplace and competitive distribution of political power commonly go together in practice, as do public enterprise in the economy and a monopoly of political power. The more the decentralization of economic power, the more likely the decentralization of political power; and vice versa.

In short, while there are some increasing similarities, there is no convergence as yet between socialist and capitalist nations at the most essential point — the distribution of ultimate political power.

9. *Patterns of belief*. We come finally to matters of belief, to the vital ideas by which peoples and societies live. These ideas include religious beliefs, national and ethnic identities and behavioral traits, and conceptions of the "good" society. Here we find great discontinuities with the other aspects of society that we have been considering. Marx never said that ideas do not matter and he certainly thought that his own ideas mattered a great deal, but he generally believed that mentalities had an economic base, although he did once write that the "tradition of all the dead generations weighs like a nightmare on the brain of the living."[51] Looking around the world, we see the continuation of religious beliefs that antedate industrial society and that have strong holds on society even beyond that of political authority. We see national and ethnic identities maintained and even, quite frequently, strengthened — Marx totally ignored the role of nationalism and ethnicity. We see conceptions of the good society divided particularly between emphases on productive

efficiency versus distributional equality, between emphases on individual and group freedom in the marketplace versus economic stability, and between "one man one vote" and dictatorship of the Communist Party as the "vanguard" of the people.

Alfred Marshall wrote that "man's character has been moulded by his every-day work, and by the material resources which he thereby procures, more than by any other influence unless it be that of his religious ideals; and the two great forming agencies of the world's history have been the religious and the economic."[52] The tools of production may be the same in industrial societies but religions remain different, national and ethnic divisions continue largely intact, ideas about the highest goals of society retain their contrasts, and even national personality and cultural traits endure. Currently, in fact, there seems to be a revolt in several parts of the world against homogenization of peoples and in favor of the preservation of their group identities. Edward Shils has recently set forth persuasively some of the "limits of rationalization."[53] Tradition is likely to persist particularly where there is no one clearly better way (for example, religious beliefs), where strong institutions are established to support it (such as the nation-state and the church), and where the innate human desire for a characteristic identity is not too costly to material results. Tradition also incorporates the wisdom of the past; helps people make choices among alternative patterns of behavior; and serves as starting point for discussion of the benefits of change.

"The mind," Milton wrote in *Paradise Lost*, "is its own place."

Selected Comparative Statistical Studies

Hollis Chenery and associates wrote a study for the World Bank entitled *Patterns of Development, 1950–1970*, which included 101 countries. They covered twenty-eight statistical variables and found standard patterns of development in each. The clearest "alternative patterns of development" were found to be based not on the nature of economic and political systems but on the external trade patterns of different countries, the size of the country, and the availability of resources. Chenery and associates made no distinction between capitalist and socialist nations; but then they included only Yugoslavia in the socialist group.[54]

Paul R. Gregory and Robert C. Stuart in their *Comparative Economic Systems*, though having severe methodological doubts about the available data, conclude that "in almost all instances, the socialist model of economic development is directionally consistent with the capitalist pattern described by Kuznets and Chenery."[55]

Alex Inkeles has long studied the social and psychological aspects of convergence, beginning in 1960 when he concluded that "standard institutional environments of modern society induce standard patterns of response." It is "man's work experience" that makes him "modern." He sees a slow "emergence of a uniform world culture" but "a very large amount of diversity throughout the world for at least another century." His continuing studies should be of the greatest interest.[56]

E. S. Kirschen and associates (the associates drawn from Belgium, the United Kingdom, Hungary, and Poland), in a two-volume work in 1974, analyzed many similarities and differences between East and West. They concluded that "now, at the end of the Sixties, there is little difference in the economic life, at home or at work, of the eastern or western manual or clerical worker, student, professor or old-age pensioner — with due account, of course, for differences in real income per capita. The Soviet plant manager, two thousand kilometers from Moscow, faces many of the same problems with his labour force, his local authorities and his far-away bosses as his American counterpart who runs the General Motors factory in Antwerp."[57]

Stephen J. Kobrin studied twenty-two indicators of social modernization in ninety-three countries. His 1975 study concluded that "in net, the convergence hypothesis appears consistent with the data." However, "one cannot extrapolate to more general statements about tendencies to convergence in values, attitudes or socio-economic and political systems in general."[58]

Thorkil Kristensen in 1974 made a study of selected aspects of developments in 122 countries, grouped into seven categories by level of advancement. He concluded: "To me there is no doubt that the trend is towards convergence, and the analysis undertaken in this book has strengthened this view." There is "no systematic difference between the recent development in socialist and nonsocialist countries . . . The terms socialist and capitalist are more relevant in the earlier stages of the typical development process." "To improve nutrition, housing, health, and education requires the same kinds of efforts whether a country is centrally planned or not."[59]

Simon Kuznets, in many writings, has found similar developments in the means of production, in income distribution, and in economic structures among many countries as they advance in economic growth. "All these patterns and trends are observable in all societies that experience modern economic growth — capitalist and communist, libertarian and authoritarian, western and eastern." He has also found that the more advanced countries economically are more likely to have a competitive election system with autonomous groups fully tolerated in politics, but says that it cannot be specified "the extent to which economic growth, once initiated, will, in and of itself, modify political structures." He sees science and technology as the great driving forces in economic modernization. His basic conclusion is that "there is a connection between the high rate of growth associated with modern economic development and a variety of structural changes, not only economic but also social; not only in institutions but also in ideology."[60]

Notations on Special Situations

The English working class. According to Marx, the workers in the United Kingdom should have been the first to seize power, since the United Kingdom was the first industrialized nation. According to Saint-Simon, they should have been the first or among the first workers to be absorbed into the all-pervasive middle class. British workers have disappointed both assumptions. Engels once wrote to Marx that "once again the proletariat has discredited itself terribly" — members of the working class had voted for the Tories; and later he wrote that "the English proletariat is becoming more and more bourgeois" and might even end up by being that great contradiction — a "bourgeois proletariat." Marx explained this on the grounds that the British working class was in the hands of "corrupt trade union leaders."[61]

Nearly one hundred years later, when even the once heavily socialist German workers had adopted many middle-class attitudes and the German socialist party had renounced Marxism, a study by Goldthorpe of "affluent" British workers concluded that middle incomes have not resulted, as yet at least, in the generalization of middle-class ways of life or of middle-class status. British workers have been only "imperfectly accommodated" into the capitalist order and are still "a potentially serious threat to it."[62]

Assuming that this is a fair assessment of the situation, and I think it may be, the question arises of why the workers have kept their class-conscious attitudes in Britain more than in other advanced capitalist societies. This may be, in part, because the historical class structure was both initially stronger and subsequently less affected by civil wars and national military defeats than in most other advanced capitalist nations, and that the educational system until recently (and still to some extent) has had a strong class bias. Also, comparatively slow rates of economic growth have reduced the degree of rise in workers' real income and may have influenced their lack of acceptance of capitalism. The British workers may still be a "potentially serious threat" to capitalism if the British economy continues its comparative decline. Class antagonisms will have contributed to this decline and, in turn, will have been aggravated by it.

But the United Kingdom seems to be the exception to the rule that workers come to be increasingly integrated into modern, democratic, capitalist systems. Exceptions do not prove the rule but they also do not disprove it. T. H. Marshall, in commenting on Goldthorpe, noted that "modern industrial societies" proceed "along paths of social change which do, in many respects, converge." Having agreed to this, we can better examine "the limits and the exceptions to this convergence," including the exception of the British working class. Opponents of the hypothesis of convergence "may reject too much"; "because a theory is not true in toto" does not mean "it must be false in toto."[63]

Industrial relations in Japan. There has been substantial debate over whether or not the pattern of industrial relations in Japan has or has not been converging on the Western model. This was a question early raised by Abegglen.[64] Actually the question should be whether or not the Japanese model and the American and Western European models have been converging toward each other. Certainly in Japan there has been comparatively more emphasis on seniority and on lifetime employment in large enterprises and on consultation and consensus in the workplace than in other advanced capitalist nations, but these practices are growing in these other nations also; and in Japan today there appears to be more job mobility and more emphasis on pay according to merit than there was in earlier times. Now that Japan is becoming the leading model for advanced capitalist development, it would appear likely that there will be more and more convergence toward Japanese practices by other societies.

An OECD report in 1977 concluded that the industrial relations system of Japan was gradually becoming less unique in important dimensions, and that other nations were learning from the Japanese experience.[65] Ronald Dore, who has carefully studied the Japanese situation, concluded that the "mechanisms . . . of the labour market are increasingly world-wide in extent," in what he calls "later late development."[66] Robert E. Cole, another careful observer, noted both "convergence in important institutional spheres" and, at the same time, "unique solutions to common problems."[67] Okochi, Karsh, and Levine reached a similar conclusion, declaring that the evidence on convergence is "mixed, . . . although surely there has been change and adjustment."[68] Marsh and Mannari observed that "convergence theory, in our view, provides at least as good an understanding of Japanese industrial organization as any presently available alternative theory."[69] Edwin O. Reischauer noted the different "balance between group and individual" in Japan, which also exists in the labor relations area, but thought that "there are signs of convergence in this regard between Japan and the West." There is "no clear dividing line between techniques, institutions, and values."[70] Ichiro Nakayama, based on his lifetime study of industrial relations in Japan, concluded that the "Japanese economy will increasingly come to look like that of other industrialized economies," and that "Japan has lost much of its uniqueness." But he said that certain traits of "national character," including "diligence and adaptability" and a strong emphasis on "preserving social order," would still mark Japan as somewhat exceptional.[71] These traits go a long way back in history: "Among the most important assets which modern Japan owes to the Tokugawa period [1600–1867] are basic attitudes like maintenance of communal discipline, dedication to hard work, desire for learning, respect for seniority and hierarchy, loyalty to communal groups, submission to authority and adherence to tradition."[72]

There still could come to be a distinctive "Japanese model for labor relations which will not take the Western model as its ideal," as Tadashi Hanami argues and also hopes.[73] But that remains speculative. Hanami writes that he is "unable to agree completely" with the concept of convergence, and he strongly emphasizes national cultural differences.[74] Even if Japan does develop its own model, that model may then become the model for other nations.

There does seem to have been "some widening of differences between perceptions of workers in Japan and the United States from 1960 and 1976," according to Takezawa and Whitehill.[75] But this seems to be more the result of new labor policies adopted in Japan around 1960 than of innate national characteristics of the workers—policy is a very substantial force and is subject to change. As a result of these policies, Japanese workers have been more positively oriented toward work, toward the company, and toward management, while workers in the United States have become less so.

My own tendency, based on visits to Japan over a period

of more than twenty years and on a reading of the literature available in English, is to agree with Nakayama's conclusion that structures and policies in the labor market are coming to look more alike as Japan studies and imitates the West and as the West studies and imitates Japan, but that there are special Japanese characteristics, particularly the individual sense of responsibility and the high degree of communal loyalty, that will make industrial production more efficient in Japan even though structures and policies become more alike. The Japanese, also, do seem to place a higher value on their human resources, which are their greatest wealth, than do other industrial nations, with the possible exception of Sweden.

Generally it would seem that the structures of industrial relations in Japan are no longer as distinctive as they were once said to be — remarkably, since Japan began with such a unique, well integrated, and strong prior culture — but that the spirit which animates these structures still remains unique. Industrial relations in Japan are certainly far more comparable with those in Western capitalist nations than they were in 1867.

China at the time of the cultural revolution. During the cultural revolution it was often said that China would develop a new model of industrialism. This no longer seems to be so certain. Mao departed from Marxism in at least three important respects: his reliance on the peasants as the revolutionary class, his conviction that the old superstructure can continue to affect the new base structure even after the revolution, and his consequent belief that one revolution that abolishes private property is not enough and that successive revolutions against the new bureaucracy are necessary to reach full communism. His successors, however, seem more intent on pragmatic modernization and even greater departures from Marx. Even during the cultural revolution, however, wage structures (not wage levels) in China were not all that different from those in capitalist nations; in fact, their similarities were quite startling.[76] China is not now the entirely new model it was once alleged to be. Paul Sweezy, then a Maoist, wrote about Russia in terms that could now be applied also to China: "The trend toward capitalism is built into the present system: control of enterprises by the enterprises themselves, coordination through the market, and reliance on material incentives — these three factors, taken together, make inevitable a strong tendency toward an economic order which, whatever we may wish to call it, functions more and more like capitalism."[77]

These three situations have been the most discussed specific possible exceptions to convergence theory. The main line of debate, however, has been over the degree of convergence between the United States and Western Europe on the one side and Russia and Eastern Europe on the other.

Conclusion

We have seen that in six selected segments of society there has been substantial convergence, but with important variations from country to country, and that in three selected segments there has been little or no convergence. The six segments that have shown substantial convergence are the content of knowledge, the mobilization of resources of production, the organization of production, patterns of work, patterns of living, and patterns of distribution of economic rewards. The three segments in which there has been little or no convergence are the economic structure, the political structure, and patterns of belief. Economic and political structures show a strong tendency toward bipolarity, and patterns of belief toward great heterogeneity. Societies can, of course, be divided into quite different series of segments than the ones used here. It is a matter of choice.

Interestingly, I have noticed a general tendency, in that part of the literature available in English, for economists to see convergence in economic means and results and for sociologists to see convergence in social patterns and behavior, but for political scientists to see continuing diversity in political structures, historians in detailed patterns of development, and anthropologists in customs, character traits, and beliefs. These differing conclusions reflect those aspects of society that each group looks at, but also reflect the inherent character of each profession, with the economist more concerned with common underlying tendencies, for example, and the cultural anthropologist with diverse tribal and cultural patterns. These various approaches help explain how difficult it is to develop a general social science dialogue about something as broad as hypotheses of convergence when adherents of each discipline look at such different things in such different ways. Political orientations, whether radical, liberal or conservative, also have their impacts on conflicting points of view.

Our discussion here shows an industrial world converging on similar means and methods of production and on common daily lives for the mass of the people, but still with great diversity in economic structures, in behavior of leadership elites, and in some forms of beliefs (Figure 2.1). It is quite

"Existence" (Marx) or the
"ordinary business of life" (Marshall)

Partial convergence

- The content of knowledge
  - Mobilization of the factors of production
  - Organization of production
  - Patterns of work
  - Patterns of living
  - Patterns of distribution of economic rewards
    - Economic structures
      - Political structures
        - Religious beliefs, national identities, highest-priority social goals

Continuing diversity

"Consciousness" (Marx)
or the "mind" (Milton)

Figure 2.1. Partial convergence on means of "existence," and continuing diversity in realms of "consciousness."

The source of Marshall's phrase is Alfred Marshall, *Principles of Economics*, vol. 1, 3rd ed. (London: Macmillan, 1895), p. 1 "The ordinary business of life" is "how [man] gets his income and how he uses it."

remarkable how the working and daily lives of the masses of the people could be so alike, and yet how the economic and political structures developed and managed by the elites could be so different. Overall it may be said that, thus far, black and white have become gray the closer a segment of society is to "existence," but black has remained more nearly black and white has remained more nearly white the closer a segment is to "consciousness."

The economic base structure has not determined the superstructure, contrary to Marx; and the life of the mind has not determined the economic base structure, contrary to Hegel: "The history of the world is none other than the progress of the consciousness of freedom."[78] Neither extreme of the existence-consciousness spectrum has emerged triumphant — neither matter nor mind, neither action nor ideas. Rather, each has had its own sphere of influence, and the existence side of the spectrum has proved to be at least minimally compatible with more than a single economic or political structure — with plan or with market and with mixtures of the two, and with monopoly of and with competition for political power and with mixtures of the two.

There are at least three points of disjunction: at the point where the production and distribution systems meet the economic and political structures, at the point where these structures face the system of beliefs, and where production and distribution systems meet these same beliefs. There may also be a fourth, where the economic and the political structures confront each other. Production and distribution generally follow a certain common logic of the industrial system. Organizational alternatives, however, stand in conflict, and here is where the battles are mostly fought. Beliefs, an inheritance from the past, impose their imprints on both the logic and the alternative structures; they constitute a cage without the iron bars.

The process of convergence that has taken place thus far in history may be compared to a series of lines that approach one another at different but also at generally slower and slower rates, and that may at some point stop approaching one another at all. Convergence may well be faster in the early stages as industrialization begins and the new means of production are introduced. Only later does it meet the strongest points of resistance in political structures and in patterns of belief. Also, at least in the early and middle stages of industrialization, socialism may be more resistant than capitalism to pressures for convergence because of its more precise ideology and the greater comparative power of its elites. Capitalism is less tied to doctrine and is, by its nature, more flexible; it generally provides for a greater "circulation" of its elites in political control. Szczepański noted that "ideological goals" can be "subjugated" in other types of industrialization, but that in socialism, ideology is a "principal and determining value."[79]

The tendencies of the past, however, may not be the tendencies of the future.

The Near Future of
Industrial Societies

3

    WHAT OF THE NEAR FUTURE — the next several decades? I raise
this question with full realization that predictions are hazard-
ous. We can try, at least, to see what tendencies are now at
work and to anticipate what changes may be likely or possible by the early years of the twenty-first century. But there
are many imponderables and, in the end, we must rely on
judgment; no one can be entirely sure of the answers. We
have had only about one century of experience with even a
modest range of industrial societies. Great Britain began its
industrial acceleration in about 1850 and the United States in
about 1890. Moreover, the whole world economic system
may be on the verge of fundamental changes. Beyond that,
some cataclysmic developments such as a nuclear war might
possibly occur.
    Karl Popper pointed out the dangers of what he called

"historicism"—of trying to predict the long-run future, particularly on the basis of one "law," since the changing content of knowledge is so essential to the unfolding of history and since knowledge now changes so much and in such unpredictable ways. However, he did support efforts to predict "that certain developments will take place under certain conditions." "For, since each generation has its own troubles and problems, and therefore its own interests and its own point of view, it follows that each generation has a right to look upon and re-interpret history in its own way." "We study history because we are interested in it, and perhaps because we wish to learn something about our own problems." It is essential, however, to be "conscious of one's point of view" and to avoid "uncritical bias in the presentation of the facts." The "merit" of each "interpretation" is its "ability to elucidate the problems of the day." "Not only" does "every generation" have "a right to frame its own interpretations, it also has a kind of obligation to do so; for there is indeed a pressing need to be answered. We want to know how our troubles are related to the past, and we want to see the line along which we may progress toward the solution of what we feel, and what we choose, to be our main tasks." This "need" should be "answered by rational and fair means." The danger comes, if and when, regardless of changing conditions, an attempt is made to find "the Path on which mankind is destined to walk."[1] But it is quite legitimate to ask: What seems to be happening within this stage of history, under the conditions now in existence and the ones that may shortly emerge?

As Robert Aaron Gordon once wrote, "We should not be afraid to keep on asking: how has economic society evolved and where is it going?"[2]

Current Forces for Convergence

Pursuit of modernization. Economists speak of "pursuit curves" in the narrow sense to mean the way in which supply and demand adjust to each other in the search for an equilibrium position. In a broader sense, many societies around the world have been pursuing the same goal of modernization, of rapid industrialization. This has set in course an effort to obtain the best technology, to mobilize the resources of production effectively, to establish viable systems of production." Societies have converged in the sense that they have met many of the same problems and have had to do many of the same things. All industrial societies must provide for law and order, create a welfare system to take care of the unemployable and the aged, control the supply of money, and generally provide a supportive structure for society; and this leads them to take many of the same actions. They have had to move people out of agriculture and into industry; they have had to educate their labor forces; and so on, almost endlessly. Central to this pursuit of modernization is the dependence of the whole world on advancing science and technology. Modernity triumphs nearly everywhere over tradition in developing and supporting the productive forces.

Competition. Societies compete with one another in many ways. The most intense is in the military capacity of the superpowers and their allies. Here no one can afford to be very far behind." There is only one best technology in any given situation and at any moment of time, and it requires production of the same materials to make it and training of the same skills to create and to operate it. Nations also compete, variously, in the sale of goods — the best automobile and the best television set; and this again requires convergence on the best engineering and managerial and sales techniques. Nations compete, too, in the standards of living they afford their people, and there are political penalties for falling behind, whether in the United Kingdom or in Poland. More nations now engage in such competition in more active ways than ever before.

Education and communication. One imperative of a modern industrial society is a literate population, with some significant proportion of the population raised to world standards of knowledge in the sciences and the social sciences. This creates a more active, more alert population than the peasant societies of the past, sunk in what Marx once called the "idiocy of rural life." New mass means of communication on a world-wide basis make it possible for the more educated populations to know of developments in other nations, and this leads them to seek to obtain what they consider better in other societies. The walls of ignorance have been torn down. People everywhere become more expectant of improvements in their quality of life and more insistent on participation in the social life of their society. The revolution of rising expectations is world wide. A more cosmopolitan knowledge within the educated elites leads to more cosmopolitan societies. Imitation is a great force in human behavior.

Common human needs and expectations. Life in industrial society requires the production for sale of many products and services; and these are much the same around the world in terms of food, clothing, health care, and so forth. There are similar preferences for better working conditions rather than worse; for higher standards of living rather than lower; for more personal choice rather than less; for an opportunity to know and to sample the cultural offerings of all the world rather than to be confined to one culture alone; for better health services rather than poorer; for protection from toxic materials rather than exposure to them.

There is a tendency in some areas to converge on certain ultimates which are almost universally considered desirable — for example, on total literacy of the population and on the highest attainable life expectancy rate (the highest average age is now seventy-six). These are, by themselves, the two best single international tests of physical quality of life, each in turn reflecting many supportive actions. It is not average GNP per capita alone that counts but also its distribution among the population and its modes of use.

A less precise and always changing but highly desired maximum is the achievable level of affluence permitted at any time by existing technology and the availability of raw materials. In 1870 a list of the now more affluent nations showed a spread in the range of about four to one in their average levels of GDP per person; now the spread is less than two to one (see Table 3.1). Eight of the nations on this list are (by 1977 data) spread closely around an average of about $4,600 per capita (in 1970 dollars), and Japan will soon join this list. This might be called the currently generally

Table 3.1. Levels of GDP per person, 1870 and 1976 (at 1970 U.S. prices) for selected countries.

1870		1977		Percent change[a]	
Country	GDP	Country	GDP	Country	GDP
United Kingdom	973	United States	5,413	Japan	1,413
Belgium	939	Canada	5,014	Sweden	1,042
Netherlands	830	Sweden	4,752	Norway	833
United States	774	Belgium	4,615	West Germany	725
France	627	France	4,602	Canada	710
Canada	619	Norway	4,563	France	634
Denmark	572	West Germany	4,414	Denmark	617
Italy	556	Netherlands	4,203	United States	599
Germany	535	Denmark	4,102	Italy	444
Norway	489	Japan	3,752	Netherlands	406
Sweden	416	United Kingdom	3,671	Belgium	391
Japan	248	Italy	3,026	United Kingdom	277

a. The percent change in real GNP per head in the USSR between 1870 and 1977 was 599 percent. Based on information in Angus Maddison, "Comparative Productivity Levels in the Developed Countries," *Quarterly Review of the Banca Nazionale del Lavoro* 83 (December 1967): 3–23, and calculations from data in World Bank, *World Bank Atlas, 1979* (Washington, D.C.: World Bank, 1980).

Source: Angus Maddison, "Phases of Capitalist Development," in R. C. O. Mathews, ed., *Economic Growth and Resources*, Proceedings of Fifth World Congress of the International Economic Association held in Tokyo, Japan, vol. 2, *Trends and Factors* (New York: St. Martin's Press, 1980), p. 7. See also Angus Maddison, *Phases of Capitalist Development* (New York: Oxford University Press, 1982), table 1.4, for somewhat different data which, however, do not change the ranking of nations in terms of degree of change.

achievable industrial standard of living. Although the range has narrowed significantly and the positions of nations within it have changed , the total range is still quite wide and the nations at the top still show to those further down what the possibilities may be. The great comparative loser over the years has been the United Kingdom; Japan has been the great gainer in percentage terms. There are pressures within each nation to reach the upper limits of what is possible, to show that it has the capability to make effective use of technology and raw materials. Each population develops the common view that if it is possible for others, it must also be possible for them. This is the great moving economic target of modern times.

These seem like such a powerful series of forces that further convergence of industrial societies might appear to be inevitable; but, as yet at least, considerable diversity still exists.

Current Forces for Continuing Diversity

Historical points of origin. The United Kingdom began industrializing with an economy already heavily involved in commerce and, as a consequence, with a substantial middle class. At first, it also had little competition. Russia and China began with largely peasant economies and under great international pressures to catch up fast with the more industrialized world. Japan began industrializing with a high level of literacy and strong traditions of careful craft work. Russia had neither of these attributes. Generally, it may be said that the capitalist industrial nations began industrializing earlier and with a more educated population, more of an established internal and international commercial network, and more of a tradition of democratic participation in political life. The socialist nations began later, with less of an educated population, less of a system of commerce, and fewer traditions of citizenship participation. Additionally, and most importantly, all of the industrial nations that have come under socialist auspices arose out of violent revolution during or following a disastrous war (Russia and Yugoslavia) or out of military conquest (Eastern Europe). China, though it cannot yet be called an industrial nation, also began as a socialist nation after a violent revolution following a disastrous war. Many of the nations now industrializing are greatly affected by their existing ratios of population to resources.

Different industrializing elites. The origins of the different industrial societies have affected the elites that have led them on to the road to modernization: middle class and hereditary leaders in the capitalist nations; revolutionary intellectuals in the socialist nations. Each of these elites, as set forth in *Industrialism and Industrial Man*, has had its own quite separate strategies for organizing industrial society. Each elite seeks to maintain control as long as it possibly can. The educational system and the mass media, on the one hand, and the mechanisms of individual and mass terror, on the other, can make that a very long period of time. The axis of industrial development on which a society starts tends strongly to direct its course of evolution, provided that its line of development is reasonably successful.

Conflicting ideologies and contrasting goals. One of the strategies of these competing elites has taken the form of a developed ideology. The socialist elites stress the power of the state over the economy and of the Communist Party over the apparatus of the state. The capitalist ideology has been less developed intellectually as a fixed creed, but it has involved a heavy commitment to private ownership of property and a reliance on the operation of market mechanisms, and has been at least tolerant of competition for political leadership. Each type of society has sought to develop a consensus around its central principles of operation. Such a consensus is essential to the smooth working of the system without the use of excessive force and with voluntarily given productive effort. Many people believe in or at least accept the tenets of their ideology or of their patterns of social belief; others find them useful to support their courses of action, whether in the use of private property or in the use of the political power of the Communist Party; and still others depend on the ideology to justify their particular bureaucratic place in the system as being useful and appropriate. Ideologies thus have their uses, but they also tend to limit the solutions available to practical problems, and this subjects them to erosion.

Each ideology has its own hierarchy of goals and there are inherent contradictions among these hierarchies. And regardless of any full attachment to an ideology, it is quite possible to have legitimate disagreements about goals. Full efficiency in production inevitably requires some inequalities of economic rewards, and full equality in distribution results in some inefficiencies. As well argued by Arthur M. Okun, "the pursuit of efficiency necessarily creates inequalities," and "the conflict between equality and economic efficiency is inescapable."[3] Also, freedom of action by individuals, by enterprises, and by organized interest groups in production and consumption stands in conflict with economic stability, defined as full employment and price stability; and economic stability conflicts with efficiency.

The capitalist combination of these contradictory goals has been an emphasis on economic efficiency and on individual and group freedom. The socialist combination has been an emphasis on income equality and economic stabilty. Janos Kornai, a Hungarian economist, noted that "it is not possible to have, all at the same time, full employment, maximum output per man hour, all-out economic growth, complete price stability, and, one might add, equality of income." Choices must be made, and they lead to different economic and political policies. This is inevitable. The idea of one single "optimal economic system" is a "wishful daydream. The choice of systems lies among various package deals."[4] There is the capitalist package, which has its advantages and its costs, and likewise the socialist package (see Table 3.2). Even after early ideologies have faded, disagreements over goals may persist not only among but also, and perhaps particularly, within nations. And different goals lead toward

Table 3.2. Contrasting goals.

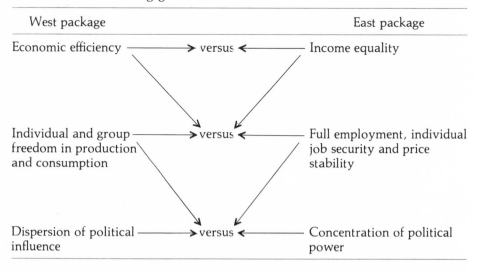

West package	East package
Economic efficiency ———————→ versus ←——————— Income equality	
Individual and group ———————→ versus ←——————— Full employment, individual freedom in production and consumption	job security and price stability
Dispersion of political ———————→ versus ←——————— Concentration of political influence	power

different economic mechanisms, and to different results. Guaranteed full employment and individual job security, for example, to which many people can become very attached, also guarantee lowered efficiency as employees are kept on and plants kept open whether needed or not. An emphasis on efficiency, on the other hand, requires more insecurity in the employment of some workers. Different people will have different priorities.

There are also political goals: to disperse or to concentrate political power. The first argues the rights of the people; the second, the earned historical right and the wisdom of the vanguard elite. Different practices become entrenched in different societies. Tocqueville wrote a century and a half ago that "the Anglo-American relies upon personal interest to accomplish his ends, and gives free scope to the unguided exertions and common sense of the citizens; the Russian centers all the authority of society in a single arm; the principal instrument of the former is freedom; of the latter servitude. Their starting point is different, and their courses are not the same; yet each of them seems to be marked out by the will of Heaven to sway the destinies of half the globe."[5]

These contrasting goals, regardless of their origins, tend to become ingrained within the people — in what they are taught, in what they come to believe in or to accept, even in what they may cherish. The American is no more likely to give up individual freedom willingly than the Russian is to give up the assured right to a job. Goals, once made sacred, can become a very powerful force for continuity.

Diverse beliefs. Different peoples also have different religious beliefs, different national and ethnic identities, and different patterns of personal behavior, and these affect individual, economic, and political behavior. These beliefs are the artifacts of preindustrial times, as compared with the new goals generated by industrial societies. They also have tremendous holding power. A religion that is against separation of church and state (Islam, for example) has clear implications for political arrangements. Heavy attachment to nationality helps draw country boundaries but also helps determine the degree of consensus within nations where boundaries are drawn on other grounds than national and ethnic identity. The traits of industriousness, punctuality, and loyalty to working communities have consequences in economic life that are quite different from those of their opposites. Attitudes toward the employment of women or of members of minority groups affect the contributions of these groups to production.

In sum, these two sets of forces — for convergence and for continuing diversity — pull in opposite directions and probably will continue to do so for a long time in the future. I believe, however, that the forces for convergence generally tend to become stronger and that those for continuing diversity become weaker. In particular, competition among nations becomes more intense while the pull of preindustrial history attenuates and ideologies erode. But there is no prospective solution to the conflict of irreconcilable sets of goals, each with its strong adherents. This, in my opinion, is the greatest barrier to full convergence. The conflicts over economic efficiency versus income equality, and over individual and group freedom versus centralized control in the economy, are likely to be eternal, with some nations putting more emphasis on one and others on another. Additionally, full convergence is greatly impeded by the ability of elites to perpetuate themselves and to continue in power.

A Multidimensional, Multiway Convergence Hypothesis

Following is a revised and somewhat expanded formulation of the convergence hypothesis set forth in *Industrialism and Industrial Man* in 1960. As did the earlier statement, this reformulation posits that the general movement is for industrial societies to become more alike.

This movement, first of all, is greatest in those parts of societies that most bear the imprint of industrialism: content of knowledge, mobilization of the resources of production, organization of productive processes, patterns of working life, patterns of daily living, and patterns of distribution of economic rewards. It is possible to specify the standard pattern in each dimension of society and then to discuss individual variations from this pattern and the explanations for them. The forces most strongly at work are the drive for modernization, the intensity of competition among nations, the existence of common human needs and expectations, and the advent of common practical problems with common solutions. The main barriers to convergence are inertia, inefficiencies, resource constraints, and the holding power of any antagonistic preindustrial beliefs.

Second, the tendency is toward continuation of bipolar arrangements in areas that most bear the imprint of the industrializing group that has given leadership to the process; these areas are economic structures and political structures. The two poles of the bipolarity are the two superpowers: the United States and the USSR, with the nations that are in their respective orbits of influence related more or less closely to their basic patterns. The two poles tend gradually to move closer to each other, particularly in the sphere of economic structures. The nations that follow their lead tend to be distributed more in the space between the two poles than in the space beyond either pole. These nations are smaller and are generally less ideologically led — they do not bear the same burdens as defenders of the true faith and are more likely to try experiments and adaptations. They find themselves pulled to some extent, but quite unevenly, in both directions.

The two poles are drawn together by the forces that leave the strongest imprints of industrialism; they are held apart by the determination of each elite group to perpetuate itself, by the conflict among ideologies and their respective supporters, and by the hold of divergent goals on leaders and led alike. Greater levels of education and communication tend to lessen the impact of these separatist forces as a world community evolves, particularly among the more educated elements of each industrial nation. But an axis of development, once started on its way, is hard to change in its direction, if only because of the inertia of complex systems.

The socialist nations are generally more rigid in their ideologies and more under control by their elites, and thus they make adjustments less facilely than the capitalist nations.

Third, the tendency is toward continuing heterogeneity in the area of beliefs.

Convergence, overall, slows down as the imprint of industrialism brings substantial uniformity in the areas where it has dominant influence; as convergence in the areas subject to bipolar solutions develops slowly; and as the limits of conduct dominated by beliefs, not subject to convergence, at least in the short run, are reached. Movement is least in those areas dominated by popular beliefs—for example, about the role of women in the labor force or the importance of hard work and frugality. But here also, cosmopolitan tendencies in the long run may reduce the hold of these beliefs.

The most impenetrable barriers to convergence are the power and tenacity of the elites that lead the process, the inevitable eternal conflict over the highest economic and political goals, and the ingrained beliefs of the people. The second of these is probably the most persistent among, but also within, nations.

To the extent that less developed countries may succeed in becoming industrial societies, they find the "image" of their own "future" in the countries already industrialized in those areas where the imprint of industrialism is dominant, modified, for better or for worse, by the beliefs of their people. They find two images of their future, each subject to many modifications, in those areas where the elites that lead the process have most influence; and these will be their major areas of choice. Many have chosen initially, at least, to try to move toward the socialist pole. Marxist-Leninist doctrine best explains to many of their national leaders the past internal exploitation of their people and the current presumed international exploitation of their nation. It gives them a personal justification for their assumption of political power as the vanguard of the future. And the package of results promised—fast economic growth with full employment and equality of economic rewards—is a very attractive one.

Depending on what they look at, the leaders and the people of less developed countries will see one or two or many maps of the future—convergence in some areas, bipolar diversity in others, and culturally determined heterogeneity in still others (see Table 3.3). Level 1 is the area of pragmatic,

Table 3.3. Diagrammatic view of three composite areas of convergence and continuing diversity.

Level 1: *Areas most subject to common imprints of industrialism: the systems of production and consumption*

Science and technology
Mobilization of resources
   of production
Organization of production
Patterns of work
Patterns of daily life
Patterns of economic rewards

Standard patterns

Variations on common themes to be explained

Level 2: *Areas most subject to opposing imprints of originating and controlling elites: the systems of economic and political control*

Economic and political structures

Bipolar diversity

0 o o o o   o o o o 0

Variations between and within each block to be explained

Level 3: *Areas most subject to varied imprints of preindustrial beliefs and behavioral patterns of the people*

Attitudes toward women
   toward work
   toward saving
   toward race, class
   toward national or
    ethnic identity and
    pride
  etc.

Heterogeneous behavior

Each situation subject to its own explanation

adaptive solutions; Level 2 of political power and of thought and of historic "laws"; and Level 3 of feelings and beliefs and emotions. There are very major disparities between and among these three levels.

This multidimensional, multiway convergence hypothesis retains largely intact the analysis set forth in 1960 in *Industrialism and Industrial Man,* and elaborates it further. It departs from the 1960 version in adding a political dimension, in giving greater credence to the continuing impact of preindustrial beliefs, and in noting that it is more difficult for industrial societies originated by revolutionary intellectuals to evolve from their more rigid ideologies and structures than it is for societies originated by the middle class to evolve. It elaborates the view, implicit in the 1960 version, that the "logic of industrialism" has more impact on societal functions in areas closer to "existence" and less on those closer to "consciousness."

The most interesting and most significant questions arise in the area of ongoing developments in economic structures and in political structures where bipolarity is now most dominant.

Further Changes in Economic Structures?

Economic structures have clearly been subject to convergence within limits, and this convergence is likely to continue. The convergence has been away (1) from colonialism, (2) from economies run by dynastic elites, (3) from monolithic state socialism of the Stalinist type, and (4) from atomistic laissez-faire capitalism of the Hayek type. The other pure form of economic structure is (5) anarcho-syndicalism, which has been tried only briefly; and it is almost inconceivable that syndicates of producers could work effectively in the absence of any state authority. At least these five alternative ways of organizing economic life have by now been eliminated from the range of realistic possibilities. Of special importance is the fact that movement has been away from the extreme forms of socialism and capitalism — a fact that is absolutely clear. This is very substantial convergence.

The problem of where to place the full communism of Marx is a perplexing one, since he himself was so unclear about it. He was very specific about what was wrong with capitalism but very vague about what was right with communism. His communism, though, may have been very close to anarcho-syndicalism. Engels, who was so different from Marx in some of his essential views, did say that production would be organized on "the basis of free and equal association of the producers" and that the whole "State machinery" would be put "where it will then belong — into the museum of antiquities."[6] This is anarcho-syndicalism.

State socialism has been subject to the following trends away from monolithic state socialism, and these are likely to continue:

First is *the use of market mechanisms,* which may well increase as services and consumer goods become more important with rising affluence, and as the masses become more cognizant of developments in capitalist nations. Also, it becomes harder and harder to plan the production and distribution of the estimated twelve million or more — and the number is rising — different identifiable products.[7] The USSR has not prevented a guided market socialism from developing fully in Hungary; and the "second economy" of legal economic activities outside the plan in all the socialist states is a market economy. It may comprise as much as 5 to 10 percent of all output of goods and services in the USSR, excluding agriculture, the military, and government. Certainly, it is substantial and growing. The "third economy" of economic activities and corruption outside the law is also substantial, as Gregory Grossman has shown.[8] Official policy now encourages limited growth of the second economy. This is true also in China. The second economy adds to output and absorbs excess income, since prices are not controlled. There is a concomitant increase in private control of productive property — although much of it remains formally publicly owned, and this tendency is further advanced as more consumer durable goods are privately owned.

Second is *the rise to positions of greater influence of enterprise managers and of members of the technostructure.* Professionals take more control of increasingly complex technologies and social mechanisms. As knowledge becomes an ever more important factor of production, those who possess it and use it in practice assume a more central position in the economy.

Third is *the continued and apparently advancing role of the trade unions* (even though they are essentially agents of the state) in the bargaining of the web of rules governing work, in the handling of grievances, in encouraging work performance, and in administering social benefits. Official policy in the USSR now calls for more consultation with unions and with other mass organizations as part of a process of moving from first-phase socialism ("dictatorship of the proletariat") to a "people's democracy," on the way, expectantly, to second-phase socialism. After the events in Poland in 1956, 1970, 1976 and 1980–81, in Hungary in 1956, and in East Germany in 1953, communist parties must be conscious of the need to keep the consent, however reluctant, of the workers and thus they must respond at least minimally to their interests. Worker efforts at control of the job have a long history and appear to be an inherent aspect of industrial production, from the job control unions of the United States, to the works councils of Germany, to the soviets of Russia for a brief period after the revolution, to the quality circles of Japan. As Saint-Simon noted, industrialism must be based upon acceptance by the workers. Marx assumed the support of the workers under socialism, and he argued that the loss of their support would lead to the destruction of capitalism. Marxist theory makes the manual workers a key class. The reality of the workplace is that the workers essentially control it; they determine to a substantial degree how hard they will work and how effectively. Political power may come out of the barrel of the gun (Mao Zedong), but bayonets will not mine coal (John L. Lewis). Without unions, without supportive ideologies, the workers can still exercise power at the shop level, and management and the state must take this into account whether they like it or not. This is true even in a gulag. Workers have enough actual autonomy on the shop floor to assert the existence of pluralism in the making of all the practices and patterns of behavior that mark the shop floor. They can share pluralistic influence at the operating levels of the economy even though their representatives do not walk in the national corridors of political power. The low productivity of workers in socialist countries is almost certainly due in part to their withholding full effort as a tactic of resistance, as a demonstration of their latent power. And unions, however impotent initially, will seek not to be confined to the shop floor but to reach out into the community, into the industry, and into national life.

Laissez-faire capitalism, best illustrated by an economy of privately owned and small-scale farm and craft enterprises, as envisioned by Thomas Jefferson and to a large extent practiced in early America, has likewise been subject to many alterations that are likely to continue:

First is *the rise of the large corporation*, with a separation of ownership and management and the creation of a professional technostructure. Berle and Means, in their classic study, wrote of the way in which owners of an enterprise gave up "power over it" until they became "merely recipient of the wages of capital."[9]

Second is *the development of the many privately based restrictions on free competition* that Adam Smith warned against two hundred years ago.

Third is *the extension of public regulations over the use of private property* — an extension so great that Schumpeter considered it a form of what he called "centralist socialism"[10] and of some forms of macro and even micro planning and of general guidance by the state.

Fourth is *the development of substantial public ownership of property*.

Fifth is *the rise of trade unions to positions of influence* at the workplace and in the economy as a whole, so that Schumpeter could speak of "laborist capitalism," and Sumner Slichter of the "laboristic state" where "employees rather than businessmen are the strongest single influence," resulting in intensive legislation to protect workers, a higher general level of wages and prices, and new contours for wage and salary structures.[11] Trade unions in most capitalist nations have come to serve as a bulwark of reformed capitalism.

Anarcho-syndicalism has been tried only locally and very briefly; but syndicalism, defined as control of the means of production by the workers, as seen in partial development in Yugoslavia and in Israel and in the communes of China, has been subject to two adjustments: a substantial role for the state in operating the economy; and a substantial role for the managers in the conduct of the enterprises.

Universally speaking, there has been an increased role for enterprise managers, for professional technicians, for workers and for mechanisms for the regulation of the use of property, whoever owns it (see Table 3.4).

The clear trend has been toward economic pluralism, toward several centers of control and influence rather than one or an infinite number; and particularly toward more of a role for nonstate initiatives in socialism and more of a role for public initiatives in capitalism. Both socialism and capitalism have been diluted. It seems likely that these trends will continue, however slowly and unevenly; that the two systems in the long run are converging "insofar as their economic aspects are concerned," to quote Tinbergen and associates. Many others have also reached this same conclusion.[12]

But there are limits. It is very unlikely that in the foresee-

Table 3.4. Evolution of economic structures.

Atomistic capitalism		Monolithic socialism
Markets ⟶	Mixed systems of reliance on markets and on plan	⟵ Plan
Private property ⟶	Mixed systems of ownership	⟵ State property
Management by owners ⟶	Control of enterprises on a daily basis by professional managers	⟵ Management by state
	Influence by members of the technostructure	
	Control and influence by workers through unions and on the shop floor	
	Regulations over use of property, however owned and managed	

able future there will be much more development of private property in socialism (alhough more public property might be privately controlled), or of public property in capitalism; or that markets will replace the plan in most socialist states or the plan replace markets in capitalism. I generally agree with Kirschen and associates that the rate of convergence in property ownership and in use of markets and plans has slowed down in recent times.[13]

Certainly, no final solutions have been reached in either socialism or capitalism. Both systems are in crisis and under pressure to change. There are signs of decay in both.

The socialist states continue to have low comparative levels of productivity and thus of consumer income, causing them all sorts of internal strains. The USSR is apparently experiencing an ominous drop in life expectancy for both men and women that must reflect many aspects of economic and social life, including standards of health care. Alcoholism is rampant.[14] The military sector takes around 12 percent of GNP and an even higher proportion of the best management, the best technologies, and the best raw materials. Thus, with output per worker at almost half the U.S. level, consumption per capita is about 40 percent of the U.S. level.[15] This is due in part also to higher levels of investment in the USSR.

The capitalist nations are experiencing stagflation on a major scale, and some of them also have rising rates of crime, social unrest, and psychological alienation. One way of measuring selected economic changes is provided by the "discomfort index," a term coined by Arthur Okun and defined as the sum of the changes in consumer prices and unemployment rates. Table 3.5 shows the discomfort index for five capitalist nations over a period of two decades.

Both the capitalist and socialist systems have a growing second economy and/or third economy that lie outside the established economy — outside the plan or outside governmental controls or outside the tax system or outside the law.

The two systems seem to be converging on internal instability, with as yet unknown repercussions.

Table 3.5. Discomfort index for five capitalist nations, 1960–1979.

Country	1960	1970	1979
United States	7.8	11.4	17.1
West Germany	4.1	4.5	7.1
France	8.6	8.8	16.8
Japan	5.4	9.6	5.7
United Kingdom	4.7	10.9	19.2

Sources: For 1960 consumer price index: World Bank, *World Tables, 1976* (Baltimore: Johns Hopkins University Press, 1976), country tables. For 1960 unemployment rate: *Year Book of Labour Statistics, 1963* (Geneva: International Labour Office, 1963). For 1970: U.S. Bureau of the Census, *Statistical Abstract of the United States, 1971* (Washington, D.C.: Government Printing Office, 1971), tables 1272, 1275. For 1979: idem, *Statistical Abstract of the United States 1980*, tables 1587, 1589.

The socialist countries, however, will certainly continue to emphasize equality of income more than the capitalist countries, through their elimination, in large part, of income from property. The capitalist countries, nevertheless, as a result of better educational systems, progressive tax policy, and rising wealth, will increasingly become more like the socialist countries in the distribution of earned income; and the growing second economy and third economy in the socialist countries add to their inequalities. The socialist nations will also continue to put more emphasis on stability in terms of full employment and individual job security, and on control of inflation, although they all have some disguised unemployment and some inflation and many shortages of goods and services.

The capitalist countries, despite their current problems, will certainly continue to place more emphasis on individual and group freedom within the economy and on economic efficiency.

In the contest between systems, the situation is now roughly as follows. With respect to income equality, the socialist nations are generally somewhat ahead. In the areas of full employment, individual job security, and price stability, the socialist nations are substantially ahead.

Regarding individual and group freedom within the economy, the capitalist nations are far ahead. And with respect to economic efficiency as it affects output per employed worker, the capitalist nations are also far ahead. The competition will continue in each of these areas. What the West seems to have, efficiency and freedom, dissidents in the East want. What the East seems to have, equality and stability, dissidents in the West demand. Certainly the West must, as it is now doing, become more concerned with its workers and their desires for greater employment and price level security, and greater equality of treatment. The East will have to be more concerned with its consumers and the goods and services they are insisting upon, and with citizens' demands for greater choice and influence in the labor and product and services markets.

In one area, the competition has already ended in a tie. The capitalist nations, while creating more welfare needs, particularly through greater unemployment, have been able to provide about as much individual welfare security as the socialist nations and sometimes more. There is another area in which there may also be something of a tie: the area of world-wide political and military power and influence. The greatest success of the USSR has been its "enhanced power and influence throughout the world." "It is under Communism that the Soviet Union (for the most part Russia) has steadily advanced in power and influence, while the democracies for all their alleged freedoms and riches have been in retreat."[16]

In summary, it may be said that there has been convergence in economic structures; that this convergence has been on pluralistic industrialism, divided into pluralistic capitalism and pluralistic socialism and pluralistic syndicalism — as in the case of Yugoslavia, each system becoming gradually more like the others; that this process of convergence is likely to continue, although currently moving at a rather slow rate; but that it will not, as far as can now be seen, wipe out differences in both means and ends. It is not by chance, however, that such great attention is focused on developments in the most mixed economies — Japan and Sweden, and Yugoslavia and Hungary.

Further Changes in Political Structures?

Convergence has been much less evident in the political and ideological area. Advanced capitalist nations all have open competition for political leadership, whereas advanced socialist nations do not. But there are some points of apparent convergence away from the pure types of control by the people in democracies and by the Communist Party in socialism.

The "vested interests" dilute democracy in the capitalist nations, and so does the rise of the corporative state. Two or three corporate bodies typically negotiate major policy decisions, with only one of these bodies subject to democratic control by all of the people — the corporatization of political life. In Japan, this takes the form of government and industry; in Sweden and Germany, of government and industry and labor. Many basic policies are negotiated between and among the "social partners" in the society.

The Catholic church and the underground trade unions currently dilute party control in Poland; and the technostructure may have some ameliorating influence on party conduct of political affairs in the East European nations. The rising technostructure can exercise, and on occasion has exercised, a moderating influence on the political and economic leadership, even giving some protection to dissidents among the intelligentsia. George Konrad and Ivan Szelényi, in their *Intellectuals on the Road to Class Power*, describe how the new "technocracy" of professionals and high-level bureaucrats accumulates affluence and influence based upon their possession of knowledge. These owners of knowledge can use their influence, their "class position," to modify the policies of the ruling political elite in favor of more effective economic practices and of merit over political preferment in the bureaucracy, and even toward protection of their friends among the "dissident" intellectuals. They can be the most important single continuing source of reform and generally in the direction of greater efficiency and more freedom for individuals. Their lifestyle does "not differ much from the life style of the bourgeois intelligentsia."[17] They do not generally make cause with the workers, however, or seek to represent their interests. Rather, they advance their own interests and are essentially allied with the political leaders; and, increasingly, the ruling political elite is recruited from the members of the technostructure. Fifty-five percent of doctors of science belong to the party in the USSR, but only 4 percent of those with an elementary education or less are party members.[18] In effect, there are two new classes in socialist society:[19] the ruling political elite that Djilas[20] has described and the technocracy described by Konrad and Szelényi. The former is dominant, but the latter is acquiring increasing influence on the conduct, the beliefs, and the policies of the party leaders.

Soviet-type governance has not traveled well outside the USSR into more fully European and into Chinese cultures. The USSR has lost control over Yugoslavia, China, and (perhaps partially) Poland, and it nearly lost control over East Germany, Hungary, and Czechoslovakia. It cannot be said that this form of governance has yet proved its endurance outside the USSR itself. There are so many leakages across the socialist borders by radio, television, travel abroad, and tourists — the border between Finland and the USSR is quite open — and by circulation of magazines and books from abroad, that knowledge of other ways and other possibilities spreads very widely over several generations, with subversive influence even in the USSR.

More generally, as a concomitant of advancing modernization in both capitalism and socialism, people are better educated, the means of communication improve, and, as Adelman and Morris have shown, there is a tendency everywhere for more participation by individuals within society and within organizations, though not necessarily in the instruments of political life.[21]

All this leaves the two types of systems still far apart in their political structures — the one committed to open competition for political leadership among rival elites and the

other to closed competition within the party. Marx and
Engels had assumed a democratic development of socialism,
once it had been achieved; but Lenin did not. He emphasized
the monopoly of the party over political power. Marx had
noted, with approval, how the workers had taken direct control over the communes set up to exercise political authority
during the civil war in France in 1870–71. "The Commune
was formed of the municipal councillors, chosen by universal
suffrage in the various wards of the town, responsible and
revocable at short terms. The majority of its members were
naturally working men, or acknowledged representatives of
the working class. The Commune was to be a working, not a
parliamentary body, executive and legislative at the same
time."[22] Lenin, however, destroyed the democratically
governed soviets in Russia, which had been set up to run the
factories, shortly after the revolution. The party took control.

Lenin saw the party as quite superior to the workers: "The
main attention must be directed to raising workers to revolu-
tionaries, not at all to lowering ourselves to the 'working
mass.' " The party and only the party knew the true needs of
the people and "we must not return to the old prejudices,
which subordinate the interests of the people to formal
democracy." Worker opposition to the party dictatorship was
called "anarcho-syndicalist deviation." "Yes, it is a dictatorship of our party! That is what we stand for and we shall not
shift from this position, because it is the party that has won,
in the course of decades, the position of vanguard of the entire factory and industrial proletariat." It is the party that has
"absorbed the revolutionary energy of the class." "We do not
promise any freedom, or any democracy."[23] This is the
essence of Leninism that gives to the Communist Party its
claims to legitimacy as based on the precepts of its great
revolutionary leader. These views have governed the position of the leadership of the USSR for sixty years and are ger-
mane to the current dispute in Poland. A recent slogan in the
USSR is "No Marxism without Leninism."

Trotsky, too, in his *Defence of Terrorism*, said that all
"questions of principle" and all "serious conflicts" within the

trade unions "are decided" by the party. "The trade unions . . . fall under the leadership of the Communist Party." He favored the "militarisation of labor."[24]

This monopoly of political power has come to be a doctrine more central to the actual conduct of socialism than is the doctrine of state monopoly to the control of the economy; more concessions have been made in the conduct of the economy than in the conduct of political life. The political doctrine of Lenin has been more controlling than the economic doctrine of Marx.

Concessions in the economic sphere have been both more necessary to make in order to get greater efficiency and easier to undertake without bringing down the total structure than have concessions in the political sphere. Totalitarian control in the political sphere has been more essential from the leadership point of view than total reliance on the state plan has been in the economic sphere, and there has been less reason to reduce it. Once totalitarian political control is relaxed, it is much harder to halt the process than it is to halt relaxation in the economic sphere if political power has been maintained. Also, the positions of the political leaders, top bureaucrats, and members of the instruments of security are more threatened by political than by economic relaxation, and there is more of a threat to law and order, more fear of anarchy. It is more important to own the army and the police than to administer directly the means of production. "Political institutions are the dominant institutions, and they subordinate all other types of institutions," wrote Jan Szczepański.[25] Additionally, economic reforms can increase economic results, creating more goods and services to share, including with the military. Political power, on the contrary, is finite, and what one group gains another group loses. The USSR clearly prefers the market socialism of Hungary to the attempted worker autonomy of Poland. The former is less of a challenge to the party internally and to the USSR externally.

The crucial issue, as of the fall of 1982, is the one still found in Poland: Can the trade unions have autonomy from the state run by the party? Do the "workers of the world" have the right to "unite" and to throw off their party "chains?" Can they be represented independently from the party? A second issue in Poland has been the democratization of political power within the party. Can there be Marxism without Leninism? Marx wrote of the "dictatorship of the proletariat," but he did not necessarily, or even probably, mean dictatorship by the party over the proletariat, or that the party itself should be dictatorially managed. He used the term "dictatorship of the bourgeoisie" to include both monarchy and parliamentary democracy — the term "dictatorship" meant the domination of one class over another, and the communist manifesto recognized that there would be other "working-class parties" than the communist alone.[26] Marx wrote, with Engels in the Communist Manifesto, that "the free development of each is the condition for the free development of all."[27]

Poland is the one place where the experiment of Marxism without Leninism might be tried with some chance of success, because it is already a dual society in the sense that, in practice, the party shares authority in some crucial matters with the Catholic church. The contest still going on in Poland is one of the key battles internal to socialism since Lenin and Trotsky suppressed the 1921 Kronstadt rebellion, waged by the Kronstadt sailors and by striking workers outside Kronstadt on behalf of "soviets without Bolsheviks." After the defeat of the Kronstadt rebellion, all power was concentrated in the hands of the party; there was not to be, after all, "all power to the soviets" — one of the slogans of 1917.

It may be that it is one-party socialism, rather than multiparty capitalism, that generates the "seeds of its own destruction" — that creates its own "gravediggers" in the form of rebellious workers.[28] It is interesting to note that communist parties have been most fearful, once in power, of two of the groups that brought them to power in Russia, the striking workers and the dissident intellectuals, particularly of the workers.

The final outcome of the Polish conflict is crucial to a judgment about possible substantial convergence in the realm of political structures and behavior. Currently, Solidarity has retained the allegiance of the mass of the workers, and the communist party was subject in 1981 to a secret ballot choice of its leaders. A socialist form of corporativism might still evolve between and among the party, Solidarity, and the church. Pending the resolution of this conflict, it must be said that if there is any convergence in the political sphere, it is very slow and very partial; but further convergence remains a possibility, at least in the long term.

A key question is whether the USSR will allow Leninism to erode in Eastern Europe without first loosening its totalitarian control in the USSR itself. For the latter to happen first may take a substantial period of continuing internal decay, given a long-suffering subject population and the methods of a police state. However, the USSR has lived with the dual influence of the Catholic church in Poland, has accepted economic reforms in Hungary and a divergent foreign policy in Romania, and did not intervene in Yugoslavia when that country undertook its own separate development.

The pressures for convergence away from one-party monopoly in the socialist states will continue, and this monopoly can be continued only at heavy cost. Populations become more highly educated, more knowledgeable about the world, more socially and politically energized. Societies become more complex and more subject to deterioration by withdrawal of effort put into or of attention given to the quality of the product or service, and ever more subject to sabotage of the product and to its means of production. In the modern economy, the worker to be effective must commit himself to his work psychologically as well as physically — must commit his mind as well as his body. This is a very important imperative.

There are intermediate steps between monopoly of leadership and competition for leadership. One is the giving of advice by professional managers and by members of the professional technostructure. This step, apparently, has already been taken in socialist states. There are pressures from consumers for more and better products and services, and from workers on the shop floor for better conditions and higher incomes; and the workers, in particular, can slow down the workings of the system drastically. These pressures have already been felt. There are groups with which to bargain, including the officials of usually ineffective trade unions. There are political veto groups, such as the Catholic church on some issues in Poland and, for a time, also Solidarity, and perhaps the military leadership to an extent in Russia. Mass actions in the streets have been influential in East Germany, Hungary, and Poland. There is also the possibility of contested elections within the party, as recently took place in Poland. All these steps stop short of competitive political parties, but it is not an all-or-none situation.

A pluralistic political situation has been reached when, at a minimum, there is an autonomous trade union movement with the right to strike at specified times and over a substantial range of economic issues, and/or openly contested elections within the communist party — which means that there is a possibility of changing the leadership against its will without a revolution, even in the absence of a two-party or multiparty system, and certainly where both exist. I believe that the two-party or multiparty system may be quite preferable, but it is not the only pluralistic solution. There are intermediate zones between full monopoly of power and full competitive sharing of power.

In practice, there is as much of a tendency for there to be a separation of interests between leaders and members in the political sphere as between managers and owners in the economic sphere. The "iron law of oligarchy" of Robert Michels ("who says organization, says oligarchy")[29] parallels what might be called the "iron law of management" of Berle and Means. Leaders in trade unions and political parties find ways to perpetuate their influence and control over often apathetic or even hostile members, just as managers find ways to get owners to "surrender" their "control over their wealth."[30] Workers and members also surrender control over their votes. As a consequence, widely participative democratic control within organizations in a democracy is sometimes more latent than actual, available for use when necessary but not always exercised. It is through the acceptance by the political elites of this latent and sometimes actual power of control by the masses that socialism might converge (although it has not done so yet) toward pluralistic modes of political control. Sidney Hook once wrote that "the slight taste of the freedoms which the peoples of the satellite countries have been given . . . will generate an enormous appetite for more—and perhaps the hunger will spread to the Soviet Union itself."[31] But this is a much debated possibility.[32]

The current situation generally, Poland apart, is that there is somewhat more freedom of expression in socialist societies today than in earlier times but only up to the point where the dominance of the party can be maintained supreme. Judging from my own experience in the USSR in 1981, viewed from the vantage point of a first visit in 1939 (a year of intense internal and external strains), it appears that professionals now talk far more freely, including discussing admitted problems and expressing piecemeal criticisms, avoiding only overall criticisms of the system and the top leaders. W. Averell Harriman, on the basis of vastly more experience, has also noted "some relaxation in the Soviet system."[33] Big changes have taken place in forty years.

The supremacy of the single party, however, still stands as the ultimate barrier to the convergence of political structures.

In the economic competition, each side can claim some element of superiority, but in the political competition, assuming that individuals in the modern world almost universally desire some control over their political leaders and resist dictatorship, the capitalist nations are far ahead. They have by far the more equal distribution of individual political rights.

Table 3.6 sets forth several possibilities for the evolution of political structures in capitalist and socialist societies.

Postrevolutionary and Postevolutionary Industrial Societies

Paul Sweezy has written of the "postrevolutionary society." This is a society where a successful revolution was waged in the name of socialism. It is now run by a "new ruling class which derives its power and privileges not from ownership and/or control of capital but from the unmediated control of

Table 3.6. Evolution of political structures.

Competition for political leadership erodes due to:	Monopoly of political leadership erodes due to:
Rise of vested interests	More insistent advice from individuals in places of influence
Development of bipartite and tripartite corporativism	
Application of the "iron law of oligarchy"	Greater pressures from consumers and from workers
	Advent of veto groups on crucial questions
	Acceptance of more open competition within the party
	Leakages across national borders

the state and its multiform apparatuses of coercion." It is different from capitalism not only in the nature of its ruling class but in the inheritance from the revolutionary period of a greater commitment to full employment, universal literacy, widely available health facilities, the complete coverage of the population by social welfare programs, and "land reform." As we have seen, socialist nations generally do have an average superiority, given their respective levels of economic advancement, in some of these categories, but by no means do they have a monopoly on high performance (see Table 2.4). So this inheritance is not such "an enormous stride forward" from a comparative point of view as Sweezy states it to be.

The postrevolutionary society, as Sweezy sees it, deprives the working class "of all means of self-organization and self-expression" and turns it "into a mere instrument in the hands of an increasingly powerful state." The USSR, in particular, has "entered a period of stagnation, different from the stagflation of the advanced capitalist world but showing no more visible signs of a way out."[34] It is neither the first-phase socialism nor the second-phase communism of Karl Marx, but a new phenomenon. Sweezy now supports Solidarity in Poland.

It might be said, in somewhat parallel terms but less brutally, that there is also a postevolutionary industrial society that never had a successful socialist revolution. This is a form of capitalism where many markets are now manipulated, where the corporative state may gradually be replacing liberal democracy, where the use of property is controlled in many ways, and where the welfare state has significantly modified the distribution of income — as a modest stride forward. Stagflation is a universal problem in the postevolutionary societies, and there seems to be no way out. These societies have moved beyond the capitalism of Alfred Marshall and of equilibria in free markets.

It is postrevolutionary and postevolutionary industrial societies that now confront each other. The revolutionary experiences of the one group and the evolutionary experiences of the other, each on the way to full industrialism, constitute the greatest continuing differences between the two. They both still carry their birthmarks, but will perhaps not do so forever. Simon Kuznets has written: "But if within three to five decades the Communist countries that entered the industrialization process first have progressed to the point where their basic capital framework is completed, and peaceful coexistence continues, the desires of their populations for greater freedom and the drive toward greater economic efficiency may bring about a dissolution of minority dictatorship, a broadening of the political framework, recovery of consumer sovereignty, and a sufficient minimum of individual freedom. At that stage — of a typical welfare state with a broad democratic framework — it might become necessary to include the Communist states in our sample of developed countries, and view them as another group of units in modern economic growth, differing in the character of their transition phases but converging toward the others as they mature."[35]

In the meantime, both types of society are in trouble and both are confronting changing circumstances. Both are experiencing slower economic growth — the postrevolutionary because of low outputs per unit of input (low productivities), and the postevolutionary because demand tends to run beyond supply, thus causing inflation, the control of which requires a dampening of both demand and supply. Both types of societies are experiencing an erosion of morale — the people never had it so good in terms of GNP per capita, yet have never felt so bad. The growth of material welfare has not been matched by an increase in satisfaction with life.

The industrial way of life is in trouble. The "social limits" to growth have meant "social congestion" in many aspects of life, and the "paradox of affluence": trying to get "ahead of the crowd" has meant that no one is really better off.[36] Industrial societies are increasingly hard to administer in their complexities. Not only "postindustrial" capitalism but also "postindustrial" socialism has its "cultural contradictions." In capitalism this has meant conflict among the egalitarian tendencies of political life, the meritocratic demands of economic life, and the self-indulgence of cultural life.[37] In socialism it has meant contradictions between a more educated populace and continued political authoritarianism, between rising expectations for material rewards and a slowing rate of growth of output per capita, and between continuing national and ethnic identities submerged by Russian imperialism. The welfare state, in both types of systems, has reached the approximate limits of its expansion (except in Japan), short of being a drag on the whole economy. There are cultural contradictions inherent in industrialism, under whatever auspices.

Centralized one-party socialism has less and less appeal in the West. The workers, through their organizations (as in Sweden, Germany, and other countries), are demanding more control over the job, the company, and even over the economy than ever before; but generally they are not demanding state ownership of property, operation under the plan, nor one-party dictatorship. Codetermination and the corporative state are retreats from and substitutes for the earlier cry for full state socialism. Capitalism has little appeal in the East. Workers there want more control over their unions and over their political leaders, and better quality and quantity of goods and services in the markets, but they are not demanding private ownership of factories. Two "gods,"

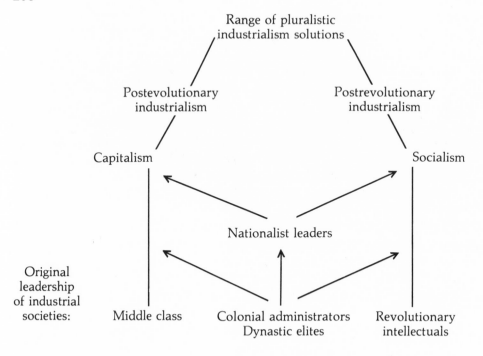

Figure 3.1. Evolution of pluralistic industrialism.

This presentation draws on Jan Sollenius, *Functional Evolutionary Materialism* (Stockholm: Swedish Institute for Social Research, 1982), fig. 11: "Probable Development Prospects for the Main Societal Types of Industrialization."

not one, have failed to attract universal support. Communism is not the only "god that failed":[38] laissez-faire capitalism has, too.

The revolutionary legacies of socialism include dictatorships that are more and more resented, ideological rhetoric that is less and less believed, economic controls that are more and more counterproductive, and promises of income equality and individual job security that are more and more stifling to efficiency. The evolutionary legacies of capitalism include a distrust of the state that often handicaps the performance of its essential functions, a worship of affluence that is degrading to the environment and human morality alike, a promise of "more, more, more, and now" that cannot forever be fulfilled, and an ideology of hedonism that sacrifices the future to the present.

The central issue is no longer just the ownership of property, as it was for Marx, or just the free operation of markets, as it was for Hayek. There is no longer one solution to all the ills of mankind.

Figure 3.1 sets forth a schematic summary of the evolution of pluralistic industrialism with its range of solutions. Each solution is marked by a substantial distribution of authority and influence among public and private organizations and interest groups, heavy emphasis upon distributive welfare, and a largely horizontal structure of interest groups rather than a vertical structure of economic classes; and each creates individual affluence.

Historical and current trends, however, may be greatly affected by basic new developments.

A New Stage of History?

4

SELDOM, IF EVER, in modern times have prospects for the future been seen so variously. They range from universal affluence to universal annihilation; from Herman Kahn, who believes that the average standard of living around the world will come to be above that now found in any nation, to Richard Falk, who believes that "despair," "desperation," "catastrophe," and "annihilation" may lie ahead, and in this order.[1]

We cannot know what the future will hold. However, the economic prospects that seem most likely to me are set forth in Wassily Leontief's report to the United Nations; the Interfutures report, *Facing the Future*, by the OECD; and the *Global 2000* report to the president of the United States. Each shows a prospective scarcity of energy sources and raw materials becoming more and more acute after the year 2000, with the consequences (pointed out by Eric Ashby) of "unresolved international tensions between nations" and "unresolved tensions within nations" developing even before these scarcities have fully materialized.[2] If convergence does lie ahead, it could be convergence on doom, or a Kafkaesque authoritarian world, or the "1984" of George Orwell, or the "brave new world" of Aldous Huxley.[3] Both continued economic growth and a future cessation of growth could possibly lead to ruin, the former by depleting natural resources and causing ruinous pollution, and the latter by leading to unbearable internal social tensions and even to war.

Much will depend on the possibilities of new technological breakthroughs, with the most likely areas for new developments being microelectronics, biotechnology, and new sources of energy. However, the introduction of pivotal inventions during the period since 1876 (at least for those that originated in the United States, which covers many of them) has slowed over the past two decades, particularly in the past ten years. "Pivotal" inventions are defined as those which are the base for "many related or 'satellite' inventions."[4] Whether or not the pace of such inventions will speed up again, we cannot know. It does seem somewhat unlikely that one century of exploration could have exhausted the basic discoveries through science. In any event, much still remains to be made of the pivotal inventions of recent times.

Knowledge is now clearly "the field within which evolution takes place," as Kenneth Boulding has said. "It is the only thing that can really change . . . Changes in knowledge are the basic sources of all other changes." And since "we quite clearly cannot predict the future of human knowledge," we cannot predict the future.[5] But the Golden Age of Industrialism could be coming to an end.

Changing Rates of Economic Growth

Scenario 1: Continuation of past rates of economic growth (as from 1950–1970). If the future lies with improving technology and rising affluence, then capitalist instruments that emphasize efficiency will be very powerful in drawing convergence toward them, since the socialist nations will otherwise tend to lag farther and farther behind. The *Global 2000* report predicts that in the year 2000, per capita GNP in North America, Western Europe, Japan, Australia, and New Zealand will be two and one-half times greater (rather than the current two times greater) than in the USSR and Eastern Europe. If this proves to be true, the economic structures of socialist states could be greatly challenged. There could be more developments like those in Hungary and Poland. Capitalist economic methods could bury socialist methods.

Scenario 2: Slow-down (as from 1970–1980) and then cessation of economic growth. Generally the rates of growth of the more advanced industrial nations have been slowing down, and the standard growth curve in the course of economic development has been from slow to faster to slower (see Figure 4.1).[6] If, however, the future lies with decreasing rates of growth, leading eventually to cessation of growth, then a different result is likely. This development will lead, within capitalism, to increasingly insistent demands for more equal distribution of income in the absence of rising incomes. It will also lead to more pressures to control the otherwise ascending inflation, to assure reasonable levels of employment, and to provide an equitable distribution of employment opportunities. Interest groups in capitalism may get out of hand, each frantically trying to increase its share of the distribution of the static GNP. The freedom of action of such groups in capitalism could turn out to be its Achilles' heel. Even when corporative arrangements have been worked out, as in Sweden, they may become unstable, particularly because the union partner is always open to internal attacks from the political left; such coalitions are inherently fragile — trouble in any one means trouble for all. This will, I believe, lead toward socialist mechanisms of distributing income and controlling the economy in the direction of economic and political stability. Socialism will be at a comparative advantage in a slowed-down economic world where capitalism is plagued by stagflation. The survival of socialism is less dependent upon economic growth, and socialist nations al-

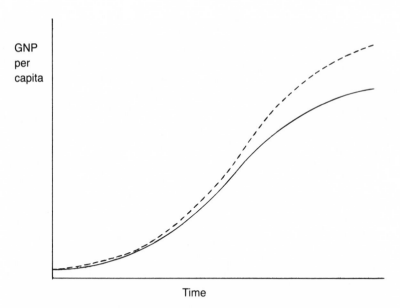

Figure 4.1. Growth of GNP per capita during economic development.

The two curves show growth over time under differing assumptions about the stock
of existing knowledge. *Source:* Thorkil Kristensen, *Development in Rich and Poor
Countries: A General Theory with Statistical Analyses* (New York: Praeger, 1974),
fig. 4.1.

ready have the more developed mechanisms to distribute income more equally, to control inflation, to assure full
employment. The socialist economies have shown greater
willingness and ability to control the economy through
heavy-handed social persuasion, intimidation, and law en-
forcement. They have much less of a tradition of freedom for
self-interest, and they also have more effective mechanisms in
place to put down social unrest. The capitalist nations under
these conditions will be subject to great challenges. At a
minimum, Schumpeter-type socialism becomes a real possibility. At the same time, however, socialist nations may re-
sort to more use of market mechanisms to maintain growth.

Scenario 3: Advent of economic decline. If actual decline
should set in, as happened in Uruguay from 1955 to 1970 and

in Chile from 1970 to 1977, then not only a heavily controlled economy but also a heavily controlled political system appears possible. Robert Heilbroner sees such a decline ahead and believes that it will lead to "the rise of 'military-socialist' governments as the only kinds of regimes capable of establishing workable economic and social systems"; the "difficulties and dangers of continued economic growth" will lead to "a drift toward authoritarian measures."[7]

The list of countries that have in recent times experienced negative growth (at a rate of -0.5 percent or more per year in per capita GNP) is a distressing one. In some cases, such as Uruguay (once called the Switzerland of Latin America) and Chile, which has the longest history in Latin America of democratic elections, negative growth helped cause substantial internal unrest. In others, it resulted from such unrest. The list includes, in addition to Uruguay and Chile, Cuba and several other, particularly African and Caribbean nations (see Table 4.1). Poland had a decline in industrial production of 2 percent in 1979 and of 7.6 percent in 1980, with a series of strikes starting in August of that year. Average real wages declined by 2.7 percent as early as 1978.[8] Even a socialist nation has difficulty handling declines of that magnitude. Costa Rica and El Salvador, with severe drops in coffee and sugar prices, are currently under great economic and political pressures.

Once an economy starts to slide, unless quickly corrected, the slide becomes cumulative. Social tensions disrupt governance. Welfare costs rise. Investment is impeded. Counterproductive policies to sustain old and inefficient industries are almost inevitable. The ablest young people seek to leave the country.

A great separation of paths potentially looms ahead — continued growth in per capita income and a slide toward capitalist economic methods, or a substantial decline in rates of growth or even no growth at all and a slide toward socialist economic methods. The latter eventuality, if it proceeds too far or too fast, could also give rise not only to internal unrest and military dictatorships but also to the greater likelihood of international conflict, as some societies might

Table 4.1. Countries with average annual growth rates of −0.5 percent or lower in GNP per capita, either 1960–1970 or 1970–1977 or both, and growth rates 1960–1977.

Country	Growth in GNP per capita		
	1960–1970	1970–1977	1960–1977
Algeria	−3.5	2.1	−1.2
Angola	−1.4	−3.4	−0.6
Chad	−1.3	−1.0	−1.2
Chile	1.7	−1.8	0.2
Cuba	−3.2	−1.2	−2.4
Ghana	0.0	−2.0	−0.8
Haiti	−1.0	2.1	0.3
Jamaica	3.0	−2.0	0.9
Madagascar	n.a.	−2.7	n.a.
Mozambique	3.3	−4.3	0.1
Niger	−0.9	−1.8	−1.3
Rwanda	−0.8	1.3	0.1
Sierra Leone	1.2	−1.3	0.2
Somalia	1.5	−1.1	0.4
South Yemen	−4.6	n.a.	n.a.
Uruguay[a]	−0.8	1.3	0.1
Zaire	0.2	−1.4	−0.5

a. For 1955–1960, the rate was −1.1.

Sources: For 1960–1970: Thorkil Kristensen, *Development in Rich and Poor Countries: A General Theory with Statistical Analyses* (New York: Praeger, 1974), table A.1. For 1970–1977: World Bank, *World Bank Atlas, 1979* (Washington, D.C.: World Bank, 1980). For Uruguay: Inter-American Committee on the Alliance for Progress, Pan American Union, *Evaluation of the National and Social Development Plan of the Republic of Uruguay, 1965–1974* (Washington, D.C.: Inter-American Committee on the Alliance for Progress, 1967); and World Bank, *World Bank Atlas, 1979.*

react in desperation. Convergence could be on confrontation of nation against nation, and region against region. The worst combination for the future would be a more or less simultaneous exhaustion of possible new technologies, of nonrenewable raw materials, and of the capacity of large-scale industrial societies to provide social cohesion.

Scenario 4: Mixed directions of movement. A fourth possibility is for a slow-down to take place in average rates of economic growth but with great variations around the average. For illustrative purposes, Scenario 1 might be said to be continuing average GNP growth rates of 3 to 4 percent; Scenario 2 of 2 to 0 percent; Scenario 3 of minus 1 to 2 percent or more; and Scenario 4 of an average of 2 percent but with great variations around this average. At an average for the industrial nations of 2 percent, instead of 4 percent, some nations with positive growth rates in the past would reach zero growth if the past distribution of growth rates were to continue. Instead of some nations growing faster than others, some would continue to grow and others would not grow at all. A great divergence could then take place between these two sets of nations — one set continuing to rise and the other remaining static.

Examples of those that might continue to rise are Japan, South Korea, Taiwan, Singapore, and Malaysia (the Kuala Lumpur district). They have had spectacular growth rates in the recent past (see Table 4.2). Herman Kahn has referred to them as "neo-Confucian cultures" with a "Confucian ethic."[9] Certainly they have shown a great sense of personal responsibility among their workers and of mutual loyalty within the producing community. Their people have a Confucian belief in the perfectibility of man.[10] Rates of savings and investments are very high. New technology is avidly sought. Government and industry work closely together.

Table 4.2. Recent rates of growth for four Asian countries.

Country	Annual rate of growth in GNP per capita, 1970–1975, in percent	Gross domestic investment as percent of GDP, 1977
Japan	4.0	30.7
South Korea	8.2	27.2
Taiwan	5.7	24.9
Singapore	7.3	33.3

Source: For GNP growth rate: Thomas Kurian, The Book of World Rankings (New York: Facts on File, 1979). For investment: International Bank for Reconstruction and Development, World Tables (Baltimore: Johns Hopkins University Press, 1980), table 3.

Japan, in particular, may have become the new model for industrial nations to emulate.[11] Edwin Reischauer says that Japan has found a "successful middle path between the extremes of pure socialism and classic capitalism" and emphasizes "the basic partnership between government and . . . business" as "a major reason for Japan's extraordinary economic success."[12] Earlier it was Sweden that was the "middle way," with its pioneering welfare state,[13] but in Sweden the partnership has also included the trade unions, which are only peripherally involved in Japan. One strength of these corporative middle ways (Japan and Sweden) is that they have a better chance to negotiate and to sustain income policies to fight inflation than do noncorporative capitalist societies. In any event, for whatever reasons, two of the great economic successes of the past century and of recent decades have been Japan and Sweden.

Illustrative of a nation that might reach a static level of overall economic activity, particularly after the decline of availability of North Sea oil, is the United Kingdom. The United Kingdom was the first nation to pioneer with industrial growth; it may now be the first to pioneer with no growth. This is fortunate, since it may well be in the best situation to make a success of no growth, and thus, once again, to show the way for other nations. The United Kingdom has a long history of slower growth compared with that of other capitalist industrial nations and has become accustomed to it. It has a reasonably adequate average standard of living and a comparatively equal distribution of income. It is somewhat isolated by its geography, but more by its mentality, from coercive comparisons with other nations. It has a long and proven history of substantial self-confidence. Also, it has been well governed over a long period of time and has high standards of civility in the conduct of ordinary life. On the other hand, it has inherited more than ordinary class tensions from earlier times, has a very unequal distribution of the ownership of property, and may (judging from the disturbances by youth in the cities in 1981) have developed new sources of tensions. And currently at least, the older political parties are splitting farther right and farther left. Nevertheless, the United Kingdom might show the way to graceful adjustment to the cessation of growth, as Japan may show the way to continued growth.

The United Kingdom, thus far, has accepted its relative decline quite well. "The British case is unique in its combination of extended economic decline and considerable political continuity," wrote Ralf Dahrendorf. "Economic decline has not increased the intensity of political class struggles." However, "the emergence of the New Right, and the continuing strength of the Old Left" may mean that "the time of the great consensus is over."[14] James E. Alt reached similar conclusions in his study of British public opinion as of 1976 (before the fire in the streets in the summer of 1981). The mood, he found, was one of "quiet disillusion" rather than "protest." Greater attention was being paid to the economic policies of the government. People were adjusting quite well in advance by lowering their expectations. There was no "breakdown of democracy." However, attitudes of "generosity" and "altruism" were eroding and there was evidently more partisanship at the political extremes.[15] If the United Kingdom does show the way, the necessary adjustments may nevertheless be painful.

Overall, in a world where some nations move up and others move sideways, increasingly acrimonious comparisons will be made.

Scenario 5: The superpowers handicap themselves. The two superpowers spend very heavily on their military establishments—reportedly 12 percent of GNP in the USSR and 5 percent, on the way to 6 or 7, in the United States (compared with 1 percent in Japan and 3 percent in West Germany). If the USSR spent the excess on its consumers and the United States on productive investment, each would make more internal progress. Also, each superpower feels it necessary to defend its principles and its ideologies, whether Leninism or free enterprise, even when this limits its ability to adjust to new circumstances effectively. And their superpower status makes enemies abroad for both countries, and increases the opportunities for political disagreement internally.

Scenario 6: The importance of small differences. In a more highly competitive industrial world where the technology is potentially nearly identical, where physical resources are distributed in world-wide markets, and where industrialism has left much the same imprint on many societies, what once may have seemed like small differences may have big results:

the percentage of GNP spent on the military establishment;
the inherent diligence of workers;
the attitudes and policies of labor unions toward productivity;
the degree of use of the talents of women and of members of minority groups;
the quality of basic science in the universities;
the degree of effective partnership of government, industry, and organized labor;
the customary retirement age;
the comparative burdens of the welfare state;
the ability to integrate youth into productive processes;
the quality of secondary education;
the level of voluntary savings;
the human relations policies and skills of management;
the patriotism and self-discipline of citizens;
the level of marginal tax rates on earned income.

Beyond the comparative efficiencies of the plan and the market at the macro level lie many micro considerations that become increasingly important as societies, in many other ways, become more alike. To use a mechanical analogy, racing automobiles have become much alike in their general conformations, and hence the slightly better spark plug or the marginally more durable tire has assumed great importance. So does the study of what Leibenstein has called the factors that affect "X-efficiency" — of how, with apparently similar inputs on a quantitative basis, the quantity and particularly the quality of the outputs can be so different. Small handicaps and small advantages loom larger in their significance.

Here, in these once seemingly small differences, is where the preindustrial beliefs of the people and their chosen postindustrial goals may add to each other to define the psychological and sociological environments within which economic activity takes place at higher or at lower levels.

Taking into consideration all the above scenarios, it is my expectation that some combination of 4, 5, and 6 will evolve (see Table 4.3).

Who will show the way? The United Kingdom once did (and might again). Later it was the United States. Then Soviet communism was called "a new civilization."[16] Later it was Sweden that was out in front (and it and the other Nordic countries may come to be again). Now Japan is said to be "number one."[17] There have been several models for economic development over the years, none with a permanent hold on that distinction; many theories about development, that of Marx being the most famous; and many experiments with development, which are still going on.

Three specific questions are of special interest. One is whether the United Kingdom will continue its relative economic decline and, if so, what the consequences of this

Table 4.3. Future scenarios relating rates of growth to direction of movement of social systems.

Toward West package	Rates of growth and likely direction of social development	Toward East package
←———	If generally high (Scenario 1)	
	If generally low (Scenario 2)	———→
	If variable among nations (Scenarios 4, 5, and 6)	
←———	where high	
	where low	———→
	If negative (Scenario 3) ↓ Toward authoritarian and totalitarian systems of the right or left	

may be. It could be, but not necessarily will be, the first industrial nation to cease growth. The United Kingdom was once the model for industrialization, including in the theories of Marx. Now it has become more nearly the great exception. The course of its future development is of concern to many nations.

The second question is whether the socialist nations, under the domination of the USSR, will be allowed (starting with Poland) to give up Leninism while holding on to Marxism. Should this happen, the world situation would greatly change.

The third question is what direction the future course of industrialism in the neo-Confucian cultures will take. Industrialism has been most successful in Japan, South Korea, Hong Kong, Taiwan, Singapore, and Kuala Lumpur. Will this success spread to China and elsewhere? The neo-Confucian ethic may outperform the Protestant ethic.

New Ideologies, New Problems

Old ideologies are eroding but new ideologies are being born. Old goals are losing their attraction and new goals are gaining support. Old class antagonisms have been dying but a new set of special-issue groups is emerging and taking political form. A new axis has been developing, at least in capitalist societies, uniting the productive elements in society — the "hard hats" among industrialists and workers — on policies aimed at enhancing the rate of growth. At the same time, there is a new wave of interest in distributive equity taking the form of greater insistence on equality of results. This has helped unite the large dependent classes of society — the aged, the young, the handicapped, the unemployed, and the unemployable, supported by some intellectuals. These are the "outsiders" in the modern society; they mostly live on grants from others rather than on earned income. Further, there are the conservationists, who are concerned with preservation of the environment on a permanent basis, who fear that a continued emphasis on all-out economic growth will wreck both the "social order" and the "ecological order."[18]

They emphasize quality of life. There are the restorationists, who want to return to earlier societal forms and patterns of behavior — to the small town, to "morality," to law and order. And there are the self-indulgents, who want their "jam today," who are unwilling to postpone gratification of almost any sort.

These five new groupings might be identified as the blue (growth), the red (equality of results), the green (quality of life), the black (restoration), and the yellow (counterculture). Alliances on specific items and at specific times are possible, particularly between the blues and the blacks, and the greens and the reds. The latter case has already been seen in Europe and the former in the United States. Each of these groupings crosses the old-fashioned class lines of workers versus capitalists, but particularly the blues; and the reds and the greens can both demand the attention of the intellectuals. Actually, society needs more production, more equality, more conservation of the environment, more of some aspects of the old morality such as hard work and self-reliance, perhaps even more "mellow" attitudes. Unfortunately, these goals are not all mutually consistent all of the time, or even any of the time. Thus, there is a new series of conflicts, more around issues and goals and less around economic class interests.[19] The vertical society, with classes above and below one another, is giving way to the horizontal society of affinity groups that multiply. A vertical society may be subject to revolution, but a horizontal one only to shifting alliances.

Each of these new horizontal approaches relates to the slackening of rates of growth and fears of no growth. The blues want to keep growth going. The reds find new arguments for equality in the reduced rise in per capita income. The greens fear the costs of continued rapid growth. The blacks are fearful of the consequences of both more growth and no growth, and want to retreat to the security of an imagined past. The yellows care least of all.

The new antagonisms, in capitalist but also in socialist societies, are not so much between the workers and the owners or the state, or even between the managed and the managers, as they are among those who emphasize production, those who emphasize distribution, those who emphasize environmental protection, those who emphasize the glories of past times, and those who emphasize the counterculture. New issues arise that divide people not so much in terms of support for capitalist methods or socialist methods or syndicalist methods, but along the lines of support for economic growth, or for redistribution of income, or for preservation of the environment, or for a return to old ways, or for a triumph of new ways. The new divisions are over goals, not over mechanisms. As old ideologies and antagonisms fade, new ideologies and antagonisms are being born.

New mentalities can change society just as can new knowledge; they can propel society into new ways.

New problems arise. Many of the social problems of today have a global dimension — the pressure of the population on resources, the increase in pollution world wide, and the threat of the atomic bomb, among many others. These lead attention away from internal national mechanisms and national performances toward global, or at least common, solutions. All societies have problems in guiding the transition of younger generations from childhood into adulthood. The faster the nation advances, the greater these problems are. Thus, the young people of Japan and Sweden are more "self-interested" than the young people of India, who are more "society-minded."[20] Alienation of youth seems to advance with affluence; so also does intergenerational conflict — even in Zurich, one of the most affluent and beautiful of cities. All industrial societies (except Japan) have problems in financing the heavy burdens of welfare that include support for aging populations. These and other problems cut across capitalism versus socialism and socialism versus capitalism. They are problems of industrialism under whatever form of organization.

These new ideologies and these new problems do not really relate to whether socialism and capitalism converge or not, and thus attention to the convergence issue might fade in the presence of these new ideologies and these new problems. But the overwhelming question for the future will be, nevertheless, the rate of economic growth or, possibly, of the rate of decline of growth; and if there is much change, either up or down in the rate of growth, then the convergence issue will become more important than it is today. The future course of the degree and the direction of convergence lies with the future course of economic growth.

Consequences of Convergence and Continuing Diversity

What difference does this all make to individuals and to nations? To the extent that convergence is toward better technology, more education, and more effective methods of organizing the economy (and it generally has been), it leads to a higher level of quality of individual lives. Convergence through competition and emulation has had a clearly positive effect on individuals. Pragmatic policies that seek to find and to follow the better middle path are manifestly advantageous to mankind. The great mass of people in industrial nations have benefited enormously over the past century.

The impact on the prospects for peace is much more problematic. Convergence away from colonialism has clearly reduced the prospect for colonial wars. But other sources of war still remain — Lenin once wrote that "while capitalism and socialism live side by side, they cannot live in peace."[21] Whether this proves to be true or not, almost certainly the international competition to assure access to essential raw materials will increase. And nationalism is still a powerful force.

Hopes for peace, in recent times, have been placed by some on convergence (for example, by Tinbergen and Sakharov), even leading some to envisage the possible "creation of a world government."[22] Given the lack of convergence in political conduct and different geopolitical interests, this seems a very dubious hope. Karl Deutsch also has pointed out that a "partial convergence" of systems may even lead to an "increase in conflict," and that only very substantial convergence would lead to a decline in the "probability of conflict." Certainly, many wars have been "fought by countries with similar social and political structures."[23] Hope has also been placed on a new world consciousness, or even religion, of global interdependence — on what has been called "ecological humanism."[24] But as we have seen, basic beliefs, including nationalism, have changed very slowly.

Our analysis thus leaves the prospects for peace resting where they are now, on the precarious base of national policies of coexistence, not buttressed by either political convergence or convergence in belief systems. As people around the world come to live in more similar ways, they may come slowly to think in more similar ways about global problems; but capitalist, socialist, and nationalist economies and political structures all have shown survival capacity and a persistence in their patterns of behavior, and this seems to indicate that they will be confronting each other for a long time to come. Past convergence has clearly led to higher-quality lives, but not yet to a safer world situation.

The greatest hope is that new technologies and better policies for their utilization will allow the continuation of economic growth in ways that do not exhaust nonrenewable resources. This will allow the slow process of two-way convergence to continue, even in political and economic structures. It will also provide time so that new mentalities, new values and beliefs that emphasize global perspectives and "ecological humanism," can spread around the planet and so that new world structures can be created to solve mutual problems — so that there can be "the third try at world order" (Harlan Cleveland)[25] and attempts to realize "a program of survival" (Willy Brandt).[26] Mankind needs better tools, better understanding of the needs of the world of the future, better structures of governance. Another "three to five decades" of evolutionary development, as suggested by Kuznets,[27] might bring very substantial changes for the better in the world situation. The 1960s, during which the possibilities of convergence were first discussed on a major scale, were a period of general optimism about the future; the 1980s started out as a period of pessimism. The earlier optimism proved to be excessive, and so the current pessimism may turn out to be, too.

New mentalities may develop at a much faster rate in the

future than in the past. People are better educated. Means of instant communication are world wide. Some old beliefs find less support in the new situation. The new doctrine of "harmony with nature" has grown very rapidly in Japan, with a balanced emphasis on both "gardens and machines,"[28] and a similar movement has grown in the United States and in Western Europe. Mankind may find that greater happiness lies more with a high physical quality of life index than with the highest GNP per capita, and may find ways to maximize the first at minimum levels of the second.

Bertrand Russell wrote in 1923 that "the important fact of the present time is not the struggle between capitalism and socialism but the struggle between industrial civilization and humanity."[29] Some new visions of the future beyond either capitalism or socialism will be required: visions of reasonable adjustments between efficiency and equality, between individual freedom and economic stability; visions of how to continue economic growth without denuding the planet of its nonrenewable resources; visions of a reasonable, if perhaps lower, level of per capita income combined with a higher per capita quality of life;[30] and visions of a new world order organized around the solution to common problems rather than mostly around the compromise of conflicts between and among nations. The world should converge on the optimum policies for sustainable growth, and on the best ways to use the time thus gained to discover how to satisfy the human spirit more effectively than through greater affluence alone, which has proved so futile; and it must learn how to organize society so that its inhabitants need no longer live with the prospect of their own self-destruction. Whether it will or not remains very much in doubt.

Appendix
Notes
Selected
Bibliography
Index

Statistics on Industrialized Nations

Table A.1. An economic profile of selected capitalist and socialist industrialized nations, late 1970s.

| Country[a] | Composition of nonagricultural employment (percent) | | Labor force participation rate[b] |
	Industry	Services	
Capitalist			
Denmark	33	67	52
United States	32	68	48
West Germany	48	52	43
Norway	33	67	47
Canada	30	70	48
Belgium	37	63	42
Netherlands	34	66	35
France	40	60	43

Table A.1 (continued)

| Country[a] | Composition of nonagricultural employment (percent) | | Labor force participation rate[b] |
	Industry	Services	
Japan	39	61	48
Austria	45	55	42
United Kingdom	40	60	47
Italy	44	56	40
Greece	43	57	36
Spain	45	55	37
Socialist			
East Germany	55	45	52*
Czechoslovakia	56	44	49*
USSR	49	51	51
Hungary	55	45	48
Poland	54	46	51
Romania	65	35	53*
Bulgaria	58[c]	42[c]	52*
Yugoslavia	53[c]	47[c]	42

a. Countries are listed within each group in the same order in which they appear in Table 2.1.

b. Total labor force/total population.

c. Socialized sector only is included.

Sources: Composition of nonagricultural employment: Calculated, for capitalist countries, from Organisation for Economic Cooperation and Development, *Labour Force Statistics* (Paris: OECD, 1981), data for 1978 or 1979. For socialist countries, calculated from International Labour Organisation, *Yearbook of Labour Statistics* (Geneva: ILO, 1980), data for 1978 or 1979.

Labor force participation rate: OECD and ILO sources as above. For figures marked with an asterisk: total labor force from *World Tables*, 2nd ed. (Baltimore: Johns Hopkins Press, 1980), p. 464; total population from *World Almanac, 1982* (New York: Newspaper Enterprise Association, Inc., for Doubleday, 1982).

Table A.2. Indicators of input in selected industrial nations.

Indicator	United States	West Germany	France	Japan	United Kingdom	USSR
R&D as percent of GNP, 1977	2.4	2.1	1.8	1.9	2.0[a]	4.2[b]
Gross domestic investment as percent of GDP, 1978	16	22	22	31	18	31
Percent of economically active population in non-agricultural occupations	96	94	90	89	97	76
Percent of adult female population in active labor force, 1978	38	31	33	36	35	46[a]
Percent of total population in active labor force, 1978	47	43	43	48	47	50[a]

a. 1975.
b. 1978.
Sources: R&D: Georges Ferne, "Is University Research on the Decline?" *European Journal of Education* 15 (1980): 338. Investment: Organisation for Economic Co-operation and Development, *Quarterly National Accounts Bulletin*, vol. 4 (Paris: OECD, 1979). Investment for USSR: Herbert Block, "Soviet Economic Performance in a Global Context," Joint Economic Committee, *Soviet Economy in a Time of Change*, 96th Congress, 1st sess. (October 10, 1979), vol. 1, p. 137. Nonagricultural employment: U.S. Central Intelligence Agency, *National Basic Intelligence Factbook* (Washington, D.C.: CIA, 1980). Labor force: Organisation for Economic Co-operation and Development, *Labor Force Statistics* (Paris: OECD, 1980). Labor force for USSR: International Labour Office, *Yearbook of Labor Statistics* (Geneva: International Labour Office, 1980).

Table A.3. Health and education indicators in selected industrial nations.

Indicator	United States	West Germany	France	Japan	United Kingdom	USSR
Persons per physician, late 1970s	600	500	700	800	800	300[a]
Percent of GDP spent on health, various years, 1974–1978	7.4	6.7	6.9	4.0	5.2	5.2[b]
Expectation of life at birth, 1977	73	72	73	76	73	68[c]
Literacy rate, 1980, for those aged 15 and over	99.5	99.5	99.5	99.5	99.5	99.5

Table A.3 (continued)

Indicator	United States	West Germany	France	Japan	United Kingdom	USSR
School enrollment ratios, 1977–78; Percent of age group enrolled by level						
Level 1	98	100	100	98	100	99
Level 2	93	70	83	93	83	69
Level 3	40	25	26	32	19	22
Tertiary enrollments in agriculture, science, and engineering, 1975–76 through 1978–79	23	40	39	28	34	63
Percent of GNP spent on education, 1976–78 (public funds)	6.0	5.2	5.8[d]	5.5	6.2	7.5[e]

a. Includes dentists.
b. Gross national product.
c. 1976.
d. Gross domestic product.
e. Net material product.
Sources: Persons per physician: U.S. Bureau of the Census, *Statistical Abstract of the United States* (Washington, D.C.: Government Printing Office, 1980), table 1579. Health expenditures: Organisation for Economic Co-operation and Development, *Public Expenditures on Health* (Paris: OECD, 1977). Health expenditures for USSR: computed from data in Imogene Edwards, Margaret Hughes, and James Noren, "U.S. and U.S.S.R.: Comparisons of GNP," Joint Economic Committee, *Soviet Economy in a Time of Change*, 96th Congress, 1st sess. (October 10, 1979), vol. 1, pp. 369–401, table A-4. Life expectancy: U.S. Bureau of the Census, *Statistical Abstract, 1980* , table 1575. Life expectancy for USSR: Recent estimates put life expectancy for men at 63 years; for women, 74 years. See Christopher Davis and Murray Feshbach, "Rising Infant Mortality in the U.S.S.R. in the 1970's," *International Population Reports*, ser. P-95, no. 74 (Washington, D.C.: Bureau of the Census, September 1980), p. 1. Literacy rates: U.S. Bureau of the Census, *Statistical Abstract, 1980*, table 1578. School enrollment ratios: United Nations Educational, Scientific, and Cultural Organization, *Statistical Yearbook* (Paris: UNESCO, 1980). Enrollment ratios for the United States: U.S. National Center for Education Statistics, *1980 Digest of Education Statistics* (Washington, D.C.: Government Printing Office, 1980), p. 97. Enrollment ratios for West Germany, Level 2: George Thomas Kurian, *The Book of World Rankings* (New York: Facts on File, 1979), table 275. Education expenditures: U.S. Bureau of the Census, *Statistical Abstract, 1980*, table 1578.

Table A.4. An economic profile of selected capitalist and socialist industrialized nations, early and mid-1970s.

Country	Output per worker (1975 U.S. dollars)	Column 1 as percent of U.S.	Average annual growth of GNP: 1960–75 (socialist), 1960–76 (capitalist)	Average annual growth rate in labor productivity, various years	Consumption growth as percent of investment growth 1950–73
Capitalist					
United States	16,100	100	3.5	2.7 (1948–69)	122
Canada	—	—	5.0	—	102
West Germany	15,600	96	3.9	5.3 (1950–62)	88
Denmark	—	—	3.8 (to 1975)	2.6 (1950–62)	69
Norway	—	—	4.6 (to 1975)	3.3 (1950–62)	81
Belgium	—	—	4.5 (to 1975)	2.6 (1950–62)	80
France	15,100	94	5.5 (to 1974)	4.8 (1950–62)	81
Netherlands	—	—	5.6	3.6 (1950–62)	96
Japan	9,200	54	8.8	8.3 (1953–71)	64
Austria	12,600	78	4.4 (to 1975)	—	79
United Kingdom	8,900	55	2.4	1.6 (1950–62)	50
Italy	8,500	53	4.5 (to 1975)	5.4 (1950–62)	79
Greece	6,600	40	6.8 (to 1975)	—	76
Spain	7,500	44	6.8 (to 1975)	—	65

Table A.4 (continued)

Country	Output per worker (1975 U.S. dollars)	Column 1 as percent of U.S.	Average annual growth of GNP: 1960–75 (socialist), 1960–76 (capitalist)	Average annual growth rate in labor productivity, various years		Consumption growth as percent of investment growth
				1950–60	1960–75	
Socialist						
Czechoslovakia	7,300	45	3.0	4.1	1.7	42 (1950–67)
East Germany	7,400	46	3.1	6.1	3.0	61 (1960–75)
Soviet Union	7,100	44	4.6	4.6	2.8	63 (1950–75)
Poland	4,700	29	5.1	3.6	3.0	–
Hungary	5,000	31	3.6	3.6	2.6	65 (1952–67)
Romania	4,600	29	5.9	4.8	5.3	–
Bulgaria	4,300	27	5.1	6.5	4.2	66 (1950–67)
Yugoslavia	–	–	6.5 (to 1973)	–	–	

Source: Paul R. Gregory and Robert C. Stuart, *Comparative Economic Systems* (Boston: Houghton Mifflin, 1980), ch. 10, tables 10-2, 10-3, 10-4, 10-5.

Table A.5. Employment and population in selected industrial nations.

Statistic	United States	West Germany	France	Japan	United Kingdom	USSR
1. Percent of economically active population (outside agriculture) by sector of employment, 1979 (early 1970s for USSR)						
Industry	25.7	39.8	30.5	28.3	33.0	37.3
Construction	6.7	8.1	9.5	11.0	7.0	11.6
Transportation and communication	6.0	6.4	6.9	7.2	6.5	11.7
Trade; public dining	22.2	15.4	17.5	25.2	17.9	9.6
Finance and business	8.5	5.9	7.7	3.8	6.3	0.5
Community, personal, and social services	30.8	24.5	28.0	24.3	29.4	27.8
2. Nonagricultural labor force, by occupation (percent)[a]						
Manual	34.7[b]	37.5[c]	40.4[d]	38.9[d]	41.7[e]	64.1[d]
Professional and technical	15.5[b]	13.6[c]	17.4[d]	9.5[d]	12.0[e]	20.0[d]
Administrative and managerial	10.8[b]	3.3[c]	3.6[d]	4.7[d]	4.0[e]	–
Other white-collar	39.0[b]	40.5[c]	32.8[d]	44.1[d]	41.4[e]	15.9[d]
3. Percent of population in urban areas (over 100,000 inhabitants), 1978 or latest year	64	34	43	59	57	26
4. Percent of labor force in manufacturing enterprises with over 1,000 employees, early 1960s	60	37	32	33	–	60[f]
5. Percent of economically active population who are wage earners or salaried employees, 1978 or latest	91	86	78	69	86	79

Table A.5   (continued)

Statistic	United States	West Germany	France	Japan	United Kingdom	USSR
6. Average hours worked per week in manufacturing industries, 1979	40.2	41.8	40.8	40.6	43.2M 37.2F	40.6
7. Population growth rate, 1978g	0.8	−0.1	0.4	0.9	0	0.9

a. Totals may not add to 100 because of some unclassifiable employees.
b. 1979.
c. 1978.
d. 1975.
e. 1971.
f. Mining and manufacturing.
g. Surplus of births over deaths, ± immigration.
Sources: 1. Calculated from data in Organisation for Economic Co-operation and Development, *Labour Force Statistics, 1967–79* (Paris: OECD, 1981). For USSR: calculated from data in Stephen Rapawy, "Regional Employment Trends in the U.S.S.R., 1950 to 1975," in Joint Economic Committee, *Soviet Economy in a Time of Change,* 96th Congress, 1st sess. (October 10, 1979), vol. 1, table 1.   2. International Labour Office, *Yearbook of Labour Statistics, 1980* (Geneva: International Labour Office, 1981), table 2B. For United Kingdom: idem, *Yearbook of Labour Statistics, 1976.* For USSR: Rapawy, "Regional Employment," tables 1 and 4. The "professional and technical" category is overstated, since it includes some persons with specialized secondary education who would count as "white-collar" in other countries, and "white collar" is thus understated here.   3. United Nations, *Demographic Yearbook, 1978* (New York: United Nations, 1979), table 8.   4. Frederic L. Pryor, *Property and Industrial Organization in Communist and Capitalist Nations* (Bloomington: Indiana University Press, 1973), pp. 185, 192.   5. International Labour Office, *Yearbook of Labour Statistics, 1980.* For USSR: Calculated from data in Murray Feshbach and Stephen Rapawy, "Soviet Population and Manpower Trends and Policies," Joint Economic Committee, *Soviet Economy in a New Perspective,* 94th Congress, 2nd sess. (October 14, 1976), tables 10 and 11 (excludes collective farmers).   6. International Labour Office, *Yearbook of Labour Statistics, 1980,* table 13A.   7. U.S. Bureau of the Census, *Statistical Abstract of the United States, 1980* (Washington, D.C.: Government Printing Office, 1980), table 1575.

Table A.6. Comparative statistics in five areas, for selected industrial nations.

Statistic	United States	West Germany	France	Japan	United Kingdom	USSR	New Zealand
1. Military expenditures as percent of GNP, 1978	5.1	3.3	3.9	0.9	4.8	12.2[a]	
2. Average correlations between prestige scores (or ranks) given to comparable occupations in six nations, mid-1950s	.94	.94		.89	.93	.84	.93
3. Personal consumption as percent of GNP, 1979	64	55	64	58	63	58	
4. Labor's share in the value of output, 1970 (in percent)	60	59	56	56	63	50	
5. Taxes as percent of GNP, 1968–1970	27.9	34.0	36.3	19.4	36.6	49.0	

a. Estimates vary from 12 to 15 percent, depending on source and year.
Sources: 1. U.S. Bureau of the Census, Statistical Abstract of the United States, 1980 (Washington, D.C.: Government Printing Office, 1980), table 1599. 2. Alex Inkeles and Peter H. Rossi, "National Comparisons of Occupational Prestige," American Journal of Sociology 61 (January 1956): 332. 3. U.S. Central Intelligence Agency, National Foreign Assessment Center, The World Factbook, 1981 (Washington, D.C.: Government Printing Office, 1981), country sections. 4. Dale Jorgenson, Laurits Christensen, and Diane Cummings, Relative Productivity Levels (Cambridge, Mass.: Harvard Institute of Economic Research, October 1980), p. 19. For USSR: calculated from U.S. Central Intelligence Agency, USSR: Gross National Product Accounts, 1970 (Washington, D.C.: Government Printing Office, November 1975), tables 1 and 9. 5. E. S. Kirschen, et al., Economic Policies Compared: West and East, vol. 1, General Theory (Amsterdam: North-Holland, 1974), p. 314. Ratio for USSR computed from U.S. Central Intelligence Agency, USSR: Gross National Product Accounts, 1970, tables 1 and 9.

Table A.7. Selected indicators of physical facilities per capita, for selected industrialized nations.

Indicator	United States	West Germany	France	Japan	United Kingdom	USSR
Per capita energy consumption, 1979 (kg. coal equivalent)	10,785	5,992	4,297	3,723	5,135	5,558
Persons per registered passenger car, 1977	2	2	3	6	4	46
Number of households per 100 housing units	97 (1965)	105 (1972)	87 (1965)	96 (1968)	106 (1965)	123 (1970)
Telephones per 100 population, 1977	74.4	37.4	32.9	42.4	41.5	7.5[a]
Radio sets per 1,000 population, 1975–6	1,882	329[b]	330[b]	530	706[b]	481
Televisions per 1,000 population, 1975–6	571	311[b]	274[b]	239	317[b]	217

a. Excludes telephone systems of the armed forces.
b. Number of licenses issued.

Sources: Energy: United Nations, *1979 Yearbook of World Energy Statistics* (New York: United Nations, 1981), table 6. Automobiles: Toli Welihozkiy, "Automobiles and the Soviet Consumer," Joint Economic Committee, *Soviet Economy in a Time of Change*, 96th Congress, 1st sess. (October 10, 1979), vol. 1, p. 819. Housing: Henry W. Morton, "The Soviet Quest for Better Housing — An Impossible Dream?" Joint Economic Committee, *Soviet Economy in a Time of Change*, p. 797. Telephones, radios, and televisions: U.S. Bureau of the Census, *Statistical Abstract of the United States, 1980* (Washington, D.C.: Government Printing Office, 1980), table 1598.

Table A.8. Per capita income from all sources, after income taxes, in selected industrial nations, various years, 1963–1971.

Country	Ratio, top 5 percent to bottom 5 percent	Ratio, top 10 percent to bottom 10 percent	Ratio, top 25 percent to bottom 25 percent
Bulgaria	3.8	2.7	1.7
Hungary	4.0	3.0	1.8
Czechoslovakia	4.3	3.1	1.8
United Kingdom	5.0	3.4	1.9
Sweden	5.5	3.5	1.9
USSR	5.7	3.5	2.0
Italy	11.2	5.9	2.5
Canada	12.0	6.0	2.4
United States	12.7	6.7	2.6

Source: Peter Wiles, Distribution of Income: East and West (Amsterdam: North-Holland, 1974), p. 48.

Table A.9. An economic profile of selected capitalist and socialist industrialized nations, early and mid-1970s.

| Country | Distribution of income among families after taxes | | | Inflation: consumer price indexes, 1980 (1970=100) |
	Per capita income of individual in 95th percentile ÷ that of individual in 5th percentile	Per capita income of individual in 90th percentile ÷ that of individual in 10th percentile	Per capita income of individual in 75th percentile ÷ that of individual in 25th percentile	
Capitalist				
United States	12.7 (1968)	6.7 (1968)	2.6 (1968)	212
Canada	12.0 (1971)	6.0 (1971)	2.4 (1971)	217
West Germany				165
Belgium				203
France				250
Netherlands				202
Japan				237
United Kingdom	5.0 (1969)	3.4 (1969)	1.9 (1969)	361
Italy	11.2 (1969)	5.9 (1969)	2.5 (1969)	369

Socialist				
Czechoslovakia	4.3 (1965)	3.1 (1965)	1.8 (1965)	126
USSR	5.7 (1966)	3.5 (1966)	2.0 (1966)	119
Poland				199
Hungary	4.0 (1967)	3.0 (1967)	1.8 (1967)	169
Romania				—
Bulgaria	3.8 (1963–65)	2.7 (1963–65)	1.7 (1963–65)	150
Yugoslavia				553
East Germany				112

Sources: P. J. D. Wiles, *Economic Institutions Compared* (NewYork: John Wiley, 1977); U.S. Central Intelligence Agency, National Foreign Assessment Center, *Handbook of Economic Statistics, 1981* (Washington, D.C.: Government Printing Office, 1981), p. 45.

Table A.10. Rankings of average wages and salaries of workers and employees in mining and manufacturing, east and west.[a]

Industry	Average rank order (from highest average earnings to lowest)	
	West, 1963	East, 1963–1966
Petroleum and coal products	1	3
Primary metals	2	2
Chemicals	3	7
Transport equipment	4	4
Machinery except electrical, transport	5	5
Mining	6	1
Printing	7	15
Paper products	8	12
Electrical machinery	9	6
Rubber products	10	8
Beverages	11	16.5
Metal products	12	10
Stone, glass, clay products	13	9
Miscellaneous industries	14	11
Tobacco	15	18
Food processing	16	16.5
Furniture	17	14
Lumber products except furniture	18	13
Leather products	19	19
Textiles	20	20
Clothing	21	21
Number of countries in sample	19	6

a. Yugoslavia is omitted from the sample of Eastern nations because its relative wage structure is much more related to the pattern in the West than in the East.

Source: Frederic L. Pryor, *Property and Industrial Organization in Communist and Capitalist Nations* (Bloomington: Indiana University Press, 1973), p. 78.

Table A.11. Public welfare expenditures as percent of gross production, 1974 and 1976.

Country	Expenditures as percent of gross production
Capitalist	
Sweden*	27.8
West Germany	25.7
Austria	25.7
France*	24.8
Italy	20.9
Ireland	20.7
United States	14.2
United Kingdom*	13.9
Greece	10.7
Japan*	5.8
Socialist	
Czechoslovakia	20.1
Hungary	16.9
East Germany	16.8
Yugoslavia	14.5
Bulgaria	13.4
USSR	11.9
Poland	10.4
Romania	6.9

Sources: Frederic L. Pryor, "Interpretations of Public Expenditure Trends in East and West," paper prepared for a volume in honor of Lloyd G. Reynolds of Yale University (1981), table 4; data are for 1976. Figures for nations marked with an asterisk are from Harold L. Wilensky, *Tax and Spend: The Politics of Welfare in International Perspective* (forthcoming), and are for welfare expenditures as percent of GNP at factor cost for 1974. Wilensky bases his calculations on data from the International Labour Organization. For methodology, see Harold L. Wilensky, *The Welfare State and Equality: Structural and Ideological Roots of Public Expenditures* (Berkeley: University of California Press, 1975).

Table A.12. Fluctuations in outputs in planned and free-market economies, selected industrial nations, 1950–1960.

Country	Total output		Agriculture		Industry		Construction	
	Method 1	Method 2	Method 1	Method 2	Method 1	Method 2	Method 1	Method 2
Free-market economies								
Canada	3.8	3.6	20.2	20.4	4.1	3.8	7.7	7.3
France	1.9	1.6	6.0	5.7	2.9	2.5	4.4	3.9
West Germany	2.3	2.2	4.7	4.1	3.4	3.4	6.1	5.5
Norway	1.8	1.6	6.7	6.0	3.3	2.9	5.4	5.0
Sweden	1.9	1.8	4.3	3.9	2.4	2.3	7.2	6.3
United Kingdom	2.0	1.9	2.7	2.5	3.6	3.3	3.7	3.5
United States	3.4	3.1	4.5	4.0	7.5	6.8	5.1	4.5
Planned economies								
Bulgaria	10.4	8.8	18.4	16.6	4.0	3.2	18.5	16.7
Czechoslovakia	2.4	2.0	4.6	4.2	3.5	2.9	6.2	5.6
Hungary	7.2	6.2	14.1	13.8	6.1	5.7	16.1	14.8
Poland	2.2	2.1	4.0	4.0	2.8	3.9	9.1	9.4
USSR	1.9	1.9	6.3	5.7	1.4	1.8	4.7	3.9
Yugoslavia	11.8	11.0	25.6	24.7	6.2	7.2	–	–

Source: George J. Staller, "Fluctuations in Economic Activity: Planned and Free-Market Economies, 1950–1960," *American Economic Review* 54, pt. 1 (June 1964): 390.

Table A.13. Nationalization ratios[a] for major economic sectors, around 1960.

Capitalist countries	Ratio	Socialist countries	Ratio
West Germany	9	Yugoslavia	30 (75)[b]
Japan	10	Bulgaria	37 (92)
United States	15	Poland	48 (84)
France	17	USSR	59 (96)
Sweden	20		
United Kingdom	25		
Austria	31		
Finland	34		

a. Ratio of labor force in publicly owned establishments to total labor force.

b. Figures in parentheses are for sectors outside agriculture, forestry, and fishing.

Source: Frederic L. Pryor, *Property and Industrial Organization in Communist and Capitalist Nations* (Bloomington: Indiana University Press, 1973), p. 46.

Table A.14. Ratios of current adjusted budgetary expenditures to factor price gross national product, 1976.[a]

Capitalist countries	Ratio (in percent)	Socialist countries	Ratio (in percent)
West Germany	38	East Germany	36
Austria	35	Czechoslovakia	33
Ireland	34	USSR	28
Italy	33	Hungary	28
United States	27	Bulgaria	25
Greece	24	Poland	21
		Romania	13

a. Adjusted budgetary expenditures cover eight functions: political administration, diplomacy and foreign aid, military, internal security, education, health, welfare, and research and development.

Sources: Frederic L. Pryor, "Interpretations of Public Expenditure Trends in East and West," paper prepared for a volume in honor of Lloyd G. Reynolds of Yale University (1981), table 3. Methodology explained in Pryor, *Public Expenditures in Communist and Capitalist Nations* (London: Allen & Unwin, 1968).

Table A.15. Economic development and political systems: percent of countries with competitive, semicompetitive, or authoritarian political systems, by stage of economic development.

Political system	Stages of development[a]				
	1	2	3	4	5
Competitive	13	33	12	57	100
Semicompetitive	25	17	20	13	0
Authoritarian	63	50	68	30	0
Number of countries	8	12	25	30	14

a. Percentages do not always add to 100 because of rounding. All Stage 5 nations are, in fact, capitalist.

Source: Bruce M. Russett, Trends in World Politics (New York: Macmillan, 1965), p. 140.

Table A.16. Selected political characteristics of countries grouped by economic development, post–World War II years.[a]

Political characteristics	Proportion of countries showing specific characteristic (percent)		
	Group A	Group B	Group C
1. General government stability dating at least from interwar or beginning of postwar period	100	46	33
2. Party system stable	89	41	26
3. Legislature effective	79	15	0
4. Executive strong	78[b]	32	17
5. Bureaucracy modern	84	7	0
6. Regime based on a broadly based representative system	84	30	18
7. Electoral system competitive	84	36	19
8. Autonomous groups fully tolerated in politics	84	31	15
9. Status of regime constitutional (rather than authoritarian or totalitarian)	84	46	32

Table A.16   (continued)

Political characteristics	Proportion of countries showing specific characteristic (percent)		
	Group A	Group B	Group C
10. Personalismo (tendency to follow or oppose a leader for personal, individual, or family reasons) negligible	95	48	36
11. Role of police not politically significant	84	23	12

a. Groups A, B, and C are distinguished by their economic development, judged by per capita product and capacity for sustained growth. Group A includes 19 countries characterized as developed, 16 noncommunist (Australia, Belgium, Canada, Denmark, Finland, France, West Germany, Italy, Luxembourg, the Netherlands, New Zealand, Norway, Sweden, Switzerland, the United Kingdom, and the United States), and 3 communist (Czechoslovakia, East Germany, USSR). The distinctive political structure of the three communist countries in Group A explains why so many shares in the column are 84 percent rather than 100 percent. Group B includes 94 other countries classified as less developed: 12 in Europe (5 communist); 21 in Latin America (1, Cuba, communist); 28 in Asia (3 communist); and 33 in Africa. Group C includes 57 of the 94 countries that are characterized as very underdeveloped, that is, having low per capita product and "little or no prospect of attaining sustained growth within the foreseeable future." Of these, 3 are communist (Albania, North Vietnam, and North Korea), and the distribution by continents is 1 in Europe, 9 in Latin America, 16 in Asia, and 31 in Africa.

b. Coverage is incomplete; number is 18.

Source: Simon Kuznets, Modern Economic Growth: Rate, Structure and Spread (New Haven: Yale University Press, 1966), pp. 447–449.

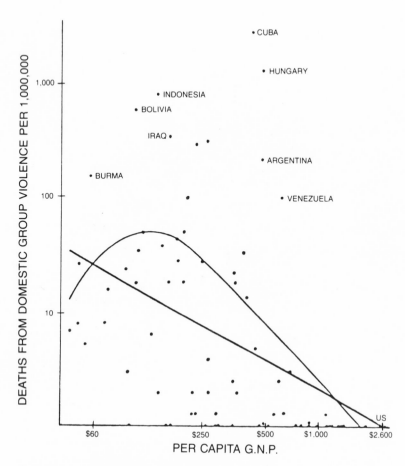

Figure A.1. Deaths from domestic group violence at varying levels of economic development, 1950–1962.

Includes deaths resulting from riots, coups d'état, civil wars, and revolutions; excludes nonpolitical murders. *Source*: Bruce Russett, *Trends in World Politics* (New York: Macmillan, 1965), p. 137.

Notes

Introduction

1. Robert A. LeVine, "Cross-Cultural Study in Child Psychology," in *Carmichael's Manual of Child Psychology*, 3rd ed., vol. 2 (New York: John Wiley, 1970).

2. Oliver LaFarge, *A Pictorial History of the American Indian*, rev. ed. by Alvin M. Josephy, Jr. (New York: Bonanza Books, 1974), p. 13.

3. Marion J. Levy, Jr., *Modernization and the Structure of Societies: A Setting for International Affairs*, vol. 2 (Princeton, N.J.: Princeton University Press, 1966), p. 709.

4. Herbert Marcuse, *One Dimensional Man: Studies in the Ideology of Advanced Industrial Society* (Boston: Beacon Press, 1964), p. 3.

5. Jan Tinbergen, "The Theory of the Optimum Regime," *Selected Papers* (Amsterdam: North Holland, 1959).

6. Clark Kerr, John T. Dunlop, Frederick H. Harbison, and Charles A. Myers, *Industrialism and Industrial Man: The Problems*

of Labor and Management in Economic Growth (Cambridge, Mass.: Harvard University Press, 1960).

7. See the discussion in Jerry F. Hough, *Soviet Leadership in Transition* (Washington, D.C.: Brookings Institution, 1980).

8. Karl Marx, *Capital*, ed. Friedrich Engels, tr. from the 3rd German ed. by Samuel Moore and Edward Aveling (New York: International Publishers, 1967), preface to the 1st German ed. of 1867.

9. Benjamin Ward, *The Ideal Worlds of Economics: Liberal, Radical, and Conservative Economic World Views* (New York: Basic Books, 1979), ch. 7.

10. Simon Kuznets, *Population, Capital and Growth* (New York: Norton, 1973), pp. 302–303.

11. For a similar description of industrialism see John Hicks, *Economic Perspectives: Further Essays on Money and Growth* (Oxford: Clarendon Press, 1977), ch. 2.

12. George Shultz, "Remarks of the Secretary of State, Conference on Democratization of Communist Countries," October 18, 1982, U.S. Department of State, Press Release 316, p. 2.

1. Laws of Motion of Industrial Societies

1. Karl Marx, *Capital*, ed. Friedrich Engels, tr. from the 3rd German ed. by Samuel Moore and Edward Aveling (New York: International Publishers, 1967).

2. Joseph A. Schumpeter, *Capitalism, Socialism, and Democracy* (New York: Harper, 1942; 3rd ed., 1950), p. 129.

3. Quotations drawn from Emile Durkheim, *Socialism and Saint-Simon* (Yellow Springs, Ohio: Antioch Press, 1958); Frank E. Manuel, *The New World of Henri Saint-Simon* (Cambridge, Mass.: Harvard University Press, 1956); Felix Markham, ed., *Henri de Saint-Simon: Social Organization, the Science of Man and Other Writings* (New York: Harper, 1952).

4. John Kenneth Galbraith, *The New Industrial State* (Boston: Houghton Mifflin, 1971, 2nd ed.).

5. Sumner H. Slichter, "Are We Becoming a 'Laboristic' State?" in John T. Dunlop, ed., *Potentials of the American Economy: Selected Essays of Sumner H. Slichter* (Cambridge, Mass.: Harvard University Press, 1961), pp. 255-262. Originally published in *New York Times Magazine*, May 16, 1948.

6. Alexis de Tocqueville, *Democracy in America*, tr. George Lawrence (Garden City, N.Y.: Doubleday, Anchor Books, 1969;

orig. pub. 1835). He believed that "the taste for luxury, the love of war, the dominion of fashion, all the most superficial and profound passions of the human heart, seemed to work together to impoverish the rich and enrich the poor." "Therefore the gradual progress of equality is something fated. The main features of this progress are the following: it is universal and permanent, it is daily passing beyond human control, and every event and every man helps it along" (pp. 11, 12).

7. See particularly his letter to Joseph Bloch, 1890: "According to the materialist conception of history, the *ultimately* determining element in history is the production and reproduction of real life. More than this neither Marx nor I have ever asserted . . . The economic situation is the basis, but the various elements of the superstructure . . . also exercise their influence upon the course of the historical struggles and in many cases preponderate in determining their *form*. There is an interaction of all these elements." Robert C. Tucker, ed., *The Marx-Engels Reader*, 2nd ed. (New York: Norton, 1978), p. 760. Soft views draw particularly on some of the earlier writings of Marx which he later repudiated, saying in the *Critique of Political Economy* that he was settling "accounts with our former political conscience." Quoted in Maurice Godelier, *Rationality and Irrationality in Economics* (New York: Monthly Review Press, 1972), p. 115.

8. G. A. Cohen, *Karl Marx's Theory of History: A Defence* (Princeton, N.J.: Princeton University Press, 1978).

9. Karl Marx and Friedrich Engels, *The German Ideology* (New York: International Publishers, 1970; orig. written 1846–47), p. 53.

10. For a careful discussion of what Marx and Engels meant by communism, see P. J. D. Wiles, *The Political Economy of Communism* (Oxford: Basil Blackwell, 1962), chs. 17 and 18.

11. Leon Trotsky, *The Living Thoughts of Karl Marx* (New York: Longmans, Green, 1939), p. 2.

12. Karl Marx, *Poverty of Philosophy*, introd. by Friedrich Engels (New York: International Publishers, 1963; orig. pub. 1847), p. 109.

13. Trotsky, *Living Thoughts*, pp. 3, 4.

14. Karl Marx, *A Contribution to the Critique of Political Economy* (Chicago: Charles H. Kerr, 1904; orig. pub. 1859), p. 11.

15. Thorstein Veblen, *The Theory of Business Enterprise* (New York: Scribner's, 1904), pp. 303, 348–353.

16. F. A. Hayek, ed., *Collectivist Economic Planning: Critical Studies on the Possibilities of Socialism*, with contributions by

N. G. Pierson, Ludwig von Mises, George Halm, and Enrico Barone (London: Routledge & Kegan Paul, 1935).

17. F. A. Hayek, *The Road to Serfdom* (London: George Routledge & Sons, 1944), p. 148.

18. W. W. Rostow, *The Stages of Economic Growth* (Cambridge: Cambridge University Press, 1960).

19. Jan Tinbergen, *Central Planning* (New Haven: Yale University Press, 1964); and idem, "The Theory of the Optimum Regime," *Selected Papers* (Amsterdam: North-Holland, 1959).

20. Idem, "Do Communist and Free Economies Show a Converging Pattern?" *Soviet Studies*, 12 (April 1961): 333–341.

21. Andrzej Brzeski, Review of H. Linnemann, J. P. Pronk, and J. Tinbergen, *Convergence of Economic Systems in East and West* (Rotterdam: Netherlands Economic Institute, 1965), mimeographed. In *Kyklos* 20, fasc. 2 (1967): 559.

22. William H. McNeill, *The Rise of the West: A History of the Human Community* (Chicago: University of Chicago Press, 1963). See also Douglass C. North and Robert Paul Thomas, *The Rise of the Western World: A New Economic History* (Cambridge: Cambridge University Press, 1973). North and Thomas stress the search for "efficient economic organization" as a basis for economic growth (p. 1).

23. Marx, *Capital*, preface.

24. Andrei D. Sakharov, *Sakharov Speaks*, ed. Harrison E. Salisbury (New York: Vintage Books, 1974), pp. 97, 100, 102.

25. Raymond Aron, "Fin de l'age idéologique?" in Theodor W. Adorno and Walter Dirks, eds., *Sociologica* (Frankfurt: Europaïsch Verlagsanstalt, 1955), pp. 219–233. In English in Aron, *The Opium of the Intellectuals*, tr. Terence Kilmartin (New York: Norton, 1962), pp. 305-324.

26. Max Weber, "Bureaucracy," *From Max Weber: Essays in Sociology*, tr. and ed. H. H. Gerth and C. Wright Mills (New York: Oxford University Press, 1946; orig. written 1922).

27. Karl Mannheim, *Ideology and Utopia*, tr. Louis Wirth and Edward Shils (New York: Harcourt, Brace, 1949; orig. pub. 1929).

28. Bertrand Russell, in collaboration with Dora Russell, *The Prospects of Industrial Civilization* (New York: Century, 1923), p. 14. See also Walter Eucken, *This Unsuccessful Age, or The Pains of Economic Progress* (Edinburgh: William Hodge, 1951). Eucken foreshadowed two themes of the convergence debate, arguing that (1) industrialism poses, for all nations that adopt it, common problems for which old answers are not sufficient, and (2) "what we

must do is to turn away from ideology and accept the lessons of experience" (p. 28).

29. Arthur M. Schlesinger, Jr., "Epilogue: The One Against the Many," in A. M. Schlesinger, Jr., and Morton White, eds., *Paths of American Thought* (Boston: Houghton Mifflin, 1963), p. 536.

30. John Kenneth Galbraith, Interview in *New York Times Magazine*, December 18, 1966.

31. Idem, *New Industrial State*, p. 394.

32. Seymour Martin Lipset, *Revolution and Counterrevolution*, rev. ed. (Garden City, N.Y.: Doubleday, Anchor Books, 1970).

33. Idem, "The End of Ideology and the Ideology of the Intellectuals," in Joseph Ben-David and Terry Nichols Clark, *Culture and Its Creators* (Chicago: University of Chicago Press, 1977), pp. 15–42.

34. Clark Kerr, John T. Dunlop, Frederick H. Harbison, and Charles A. Myers, *Industrialism and Industrial Man: The Problems of Labor and Management in Economic Growth* (Cambridge, Mass.: Harvard University Press, 1960).

35. Clark Kerr, *Marshall, Marx and Modern Times: The Multi-Dimensional Society* (Cambridge: Cambridge University Press, 1969). For a description of a pluralistic vision of socialism, see Branko Horvat, *The Political Economy of Socialism* (Armonk, N.Y.: M. E. Sharpe, 1982), p. 508.

36. Alec Nove, *The Soviet Economic System* (London: Allen & Unwin, 1977), ch. 3. The centralization is by the government; and the pluralism includes the "ministerial empires, " the "republics and the regions," and the "nationalities," each with some partial autonomy. Nove also notes the "many uncontrollable forces," the "tensions and the conflicts" (p. 167), and the "contradictory elements," including the "intelligentsia" (p. 199), that are "leading to social change."

37. Clark Kerr, "Industrial Relations and the Liberal Pluralist," in Kerr, *Labor and Management in Industrial Society* (New York: Doubleday, Anchor Books, 1964). First published in the *Proceedings Seventh Annual Meeting, 1954*, Industrial Relations Research Association, pub. no. 14, 1955, pp. 2-16.

38. Zbigniew Brzezinski and Samuel P. Huntington, *Political Power: USA/USSR* (New York: Viking, 1964). Quoted in Gregory Grossman, *Economic Systems* (Englewood Cliffs, N.J.: Prentice-Hall, 1974, 2nd ed.), p. 176.

39. Max Weber, *Economy and Society*, ed. Guenther Roth and Claus Wittich (New York: Bedminister Press, 1968), p. 223; *Gesam-*

melte Politische Schriften (Munich, 1921), quoted in Richard Pipes, "Max Weber and Russia," *World Politics* 7 (April 1955): 377.

40. Talcott Parsons, "Evolutionary Universals in Society," *American Sociological Review* 29 (June 1964): 339–357. "The rigid opposition between a 'free enterprise' system, with minimal social and governmental controls, and 'socialism,' with government ownership and control of *all* the principal means of production, has proved to be unrealistic. The emerging pattern corresponds to a general modern trend toward structural differentiation and pluralization." Parsons, *The System of Modern Societies* (Englewood Cliffs, N.J.: Prentice-Hall, 1971), p. 106.

41. Maria Hirszowicz, *The Bureaucratic Leviathan: A Study in the Sociology of Communism* (Oxford: Robertson, 1980), p. 16.

42. Galbraith, *New Industrial State*, pp. 33, 108, 150, 399.

43. James Burnham, *The Managerial Revolution* (New York: John Day, 1941), pp. 71–72.

44. Peter Drucker, *The New Society: The Anatomy of the Industrial Order* (New York: Harper, 1950), p. 203.

45. David Granick, *The Red Executive: A Study of the Organization Man in Russian Industry* (Garden City, N.Y.: Doubleday, 1960), p. 319.

46. Frederick Harbison and Charles A. Myers, *Management in the Industrial World* (New York: McGraw-Hill, 1959), ch. 4.

47. Leon Gouré, Foy D. Kohler, Richard Soll, and Annette Stiefbold, *Convergence of Communism and Capitalism: The Soviet View* (Miami: Center for Advanced International Studies, University of Miami, 1973).

48. Iu Kashlev, "Tactics of the Doomed: How the West Tries to Modernize the Old Doctrine of Ideological Subversion," *Izvestiia*, August 19, 1969. Cited in Gouré et al., *Convergence*, p. 52.

49. Paul M. Sweezy and Charles Bettelheim, *On the Transition to Socialism* (New York: Monthly Review Press, 1971), p. 118.

50. Wlodzimierz Brus, "Can Anything Be Said About the Direction of Change of Economic Systems?" paper presented at the 500th Anniversary of the University of Uppsala, Sweden, 1977.

51. Schumpeter, *Capitalism*, pp. 12–13, 182.

52. Bertram D. Wolfe, "A Historian Looks at the Convergence Theory," in Paul Kurtz, ed., *Sidney Hook and the Contemporary World: Essays on the Pragmatic Intelligence* (New York: John Day, 1968), p. 70.

53. Idem, *An Ideology in Power* (New York: Stein and Day, 1969), pp. 393–394.

54. Zbigniew K. Brzezinski, *The Soviet Bloc: Unity and Conflict* (Cambridge, Mass.: Harvard University Press, 1967, 2nd ed.), ch. 19.

55. Alexander Gerschenkron, *Economic Backwardness in Historical Perspective* (Cambridge, Mass.: Harvard University Press, 1962), pp. 191, 193; idem, *Continuity in History and Other Essays* (Cambridge, Mass.: Harvard University Press, 1968), p. 495.

56. Frederic L. Pryor, *Property and Industrial Organization in Communist and Capitalist Nations* (Bloomington, Ind.: Indiana University Press, 1973), p. 436.

57. Wilbert E. Moore, *World Modernization: The Limits of Convergence* (New York: Elsevier, 1979), pp. 150, 156–157.

58. Pryor, *Property and Industrial Organization*, pp. 367–370.

59. V. I. Lenin, "Extracts from Lenin's *The State and Revolution*" (August–September 1917), in Karl Marx, *Critique of the Gotha Programme* (New York: International Publishers, 1938), pp. 83, 80.

60. Schumpeter, *Capitalism*, p. 167.

61. H. Linnemann, J. P. Pronk, and J. Tinbergen, "Convergence of Economic Systems in East and West," in Morris Bornstein and Daniel R. Fusfeld, eds., *The Soviet Economy: A Book of Readings*, 3rd ed. (Homewood, Ill.: Richard D. Irwin, 1970), pp. 441, 457.

62. Michael Ellman, "Against Convergence," *Cambridge Journal of Economics* 4 (September 1980): 199–210. See also the discussion in A. W. Coats and S. Thompstone, "Against 'Against Convergence,'" and "Reply" by Michael Ellman, in *Cambridge Journal of Economics* 5 (December 1981): 383–389. In the reply, Ellman says that Tinbergen (in *Civis Mundi*, November 1980) now believes that convergence theory is "uninteresting from a practical point of view," apparently because of (at least in part) the lack of success of the Kosygin reforms in the USSR and the renewal of military confrontation between the superpowers.

63. John T. Dunlop, Frederick H. Harbison, Clark Kerr, and Charles A. Myers, *Industrialism and Industrial Man Reconsidered* (Princeton, N.J.: Industrial Relations Section, Princeton University, 1975), p. 29.

64. Kerr, et al., *Industrialism and Industrial Man*, p. 232.

65. Moore, *World Modernization*, p. 28.

66. Clark Kerr, "Changing Social Structures," in W. E. Moore and A. S. Feldman, eds., *Labor Commitment and Social Change in Developing Areas* (New York: Social Science Research Council, 1969), pp. 348–359.

2. Evidence on Convergence and Continuing Diversity

1. Benjamin Ward, *The Ideal Worlds of Economics: Liberal, Radical, and Conservative Economic World Views* (New York: Basic Books, 1979), p. 19.

2. Alastair McAuley, *Economic Welfare in the Soviet Union: Poverty, Living Standards, and Inequality* (Madison, Wis.: University of Wisconsin Press, 1979), p. 109. See also, for other countries, the discussion in Paul Bairoch and Maurice Levy-LeBoyer, eds., *Disparities in Economic Development since the Industrial Revolution* (London: Macmillan, 1981).

3. Frederic L. Pryor, *Property and Industrial Organization in Communist and Capitalist Nations* (Bloomington, Ind.: Indiana University Press, 1973), p. 371.

4. Jan Szczepański, "Early Stages of Socialist Industrialization and Changes in Social Class Structure," in Kazimierz Sloczyński and Tadeusz Krauze, eds., *Class Structure and Social Mobility in Poland* (White Plains, N.Y.: M. E. Sharpe, 1978), p. 12.

5. Morris David Morris, *Measuring the Condition of the World's Poor: The Physical Quality of Life Index* (New York: Pergamon Press, for the Overseas Development Council 1979). For different data that point in the same general direction, see Branko Horvat, *The Political Economy of Socialism* (Armonk, N.Y.: M. E. Sharpe, 1982). Horvat concludes that, in what he calls "étatist societies," "the broad masses of people live longer, receive more education, and enjoy much better medical care than would occur generally under alternative social arrangements at the same level of economic development" (p. 49).

6. Szczepański, "Early Stages," p. 11.

7. Alfred Marshall, *Principles of Economics*, 8th ed., bk. 4 (New York: Macmillan, 1920), p. 138.

8. Harrison Brown, *Learning How to Live in a Technological Society* (Tokyo: Simul Press, 1979).

9. Daniel Bell, *The Coming of Post-Industrial Society: A Venture in Social Forecasting* (New York: Basic Books, 1973), p. 114.

10. Karl Marx, *Introduction to the Critique of Political Economy*, suppl. to *A Contribution to the Critique of Political Economy* (Chicago: Charles H. Kerr, 1904; orig. pub. 1859), p. 265.

11. Michael Boretsky, "The Role of Innovation,"*Challenge* 23 (November–December 1980): 9–15.

12. E. S. Kirschen, ed., *Economic Policies Compared, West and East*, vol. 1 (Amsterdam: North-Holland, 1974), p. 290.

13. Dale W. Jorgenson and Mieko Nishimizu, *Sectoral Differences in Levels of Technology: An International Comparison Between the United States and Japan, 1955–1972*, paper prepared for the North American Summer Meeting of Econometric Society, Montreal, June 27–30, 1979.

14. Michael Boretsky, "Comparative Progress in Technology, Productivity, and Economic Efficiency: U.S.S.R. versus U.S.A.," in Joint Economic Committee, *New Directions in the Soviet Economy*, 89th Congress, 2nd sess. (Washington, D.C.: Government Printing Office, 1966), pt. II-A, p. 149.

15. Organisation for Economic Co-operation and Development, *Labor Force Statistics* (Paris: OECD, 1980). For Muslim countries, see International Labour Office, *Labour Force Estimates and Projections, 1950–2000* (Geneva: International Labour Office, 1977).

16. For a discussion of the differences between productivity and efficiency, see Abram Bergson, "Comparative Productivity and Efficiency in the USA and the USSR," and Evsey Domar, "On the Measurement of Comparative Efficiency," in Alexander Eckstein, ed., *Comparison of Economic Systems: Theoretical and Methodological Approaches* (Berkeley: University of California Press, 1971), pp. 161–218 and 219–233.

17. Harvey Leibenstein, *Beyond Economic Man* (Cambridge, Mass.: Harvard University Press, 1976); and idem, "X-Efficiency: From Concept to Theory," *Challenge* 22 (September–October 1979): 13–22. See also idem, *General X-Efficiency Theory and Economic Development* (London: Oxford University Press, 1978).

18. Paul Gregory, *Socialist and Nonsocialist Industrialization Patterns: A Comparative Appraisal* (New York: Praeger, 1970), p. 128.

19. Guy Ofer, *The Service Sector in Soviet Economic Growth* (Cambridge, Mass.: Harvard University Press, 1973), p. 161.

20. Ibid., p. 165. Thad Alton has also noted, with respect to "the sectoral composition of employment and national product," that "the countries of Eastern Europe are becoming more like the Western countries, although considerable disparities still exist among the countries in each group and between the two groups." See Alton, "Comparative Structure and Growth of Economic Activity in Eastern Europe," *East European Economies Post-Helsinki*, U.S. Congress, Joint Economic Committee Papers, September 1977, p. 236.

21. Elizabeth Garnsey, "Occupational Structure in Industrialized Societies: Some Notes on the Convergence Thesis in the Light of Soviet Experience," *Sociology* 9 (September 1975): 437–458.

22. Alec Nove, *Economic Rationality and Soviet Politics* (New York: Praeger, 1964), pp. 268, 271.

23. Seymour Martin Lipset, "Social Mobility and Equal Opportunity," *Public Interest* 29 (Fall 1972): 100, 196. See also the discussion in Anthony Heath, *Social Mobility* (Glasgow: Fontana Paperbacks, 1981). He calculates manual to nonmanual mobility at 31.6 percent in fourteen capitalist nations and at 30.2 percent in five socialist nations (p. 203).

24. Murray Yanowitch, *Social and Economic Inequality in the Soviet Union: Six Studies* (White Plains, N.Y.: M. E. Sharpe, 1977), p. xiii. See also M. N. Rutkevich and F. R. Filippov, "Social Sources of Recruitment of the Intelligentsia," in Murray Yanowitch and Wesley A. Fisher, eds., *Social Stratification and Mobility in the USSR* (White Plains, N.Y.: International Arts and Sciences Press, 1973), pp. 241–274. Rutkevich and Filippov show proportionately 2.5 to 3.0 times as many admissions of children of "mental workers" over manual workers to tertiary institutions of education, and particularly in medical and science programs, in the Sverdlovsk region of the USSR. Seymour Martin Lipset in the same volume (p. 381) notes "repeated patterns of convergence . . . in findings and interpretation between Soviet and Western sociologists dealing with stratification."

25. Lewis Mumford, quoted in "Putting Time in its Place," in Tommy Carlstein, Don Parkes and Nigel Thrift, eds., *Making Sense of Time*, vol. 1 of *Timing Space and Spacing Time* (London: Edward Arnold, 1978), p. 125.

26. Clark Kerr and Abraham Siegel, "The Structuring of the Labor Force in Industrial Society: New Dimensions and New Questions," *Industrial and Labor Relations Review* 8 (January 1955): 151–168.

27. Friedrich Engels, "On Authority," in Robert C. Tucker, ed., *The Marx-Engels Reader*, 2nd ed. (New York: Norton, 1978; written 1872), p. 731.

28. For a discussion of industrial cultures see John T. Dunlop, *Industrial Relations Systems* (New York: Holt, 1958), ch. 5.

29. John D. Durand, *The Labor Force in Economic Devlopment* (Princeton, N.J.: Princeton University Press, 1975), pp. 26–27.

30. Frederic L. Pryor, "Some Costs and Benefits of Markets: An Empirical Study," *Quarterly Journal of Economics* 91 (February 1977): 81–102.

31. Alexander Szalai, *The Use of Time* (The Hague: Mouton, 1972), pp. 113, 116; and idem, "Continental Report," in *Free Time*

and Self-Fulfillment (Brussels: Fondation van Clé, 1976), pp. 44, 49.

32. Soedjatmoko, *Development and Freedom* (Tokyo: Simul Press, 1980).

33. Joseph A. Schumpeter, *Capitalism, Socialism, and Democracy* (New York: Harper, 1942; 3rd ed., 1950), p. 203.

34. Marion J. Levy, Jr., *Modernization: Latecomers and Survivors* (New York: Basic Books, 1972), p. 148.

35. Hollis Chenery and Moises Syrquin, with the assistance of Hazel Elkington, *Patterns of Development, 1950–1970* (New York: Oxford University Press, for the World Bank, 1975), p. 60.

36. Pryor, *Property and Industrial Organization*, p. 72.

37. Paul R. Gregory and Robert C. Stuart, *Comparative Economic Systems* (Boston: Houghton Mifflin, 1980), p. 390.

38. Dunlop, *Industrial Relations Systems*, p. 361.

39. Henry Phelps Brown, *The Inequality of Pay* (Berkeley: University of California Press, 1977), p. 65.

40. McAuley, *Economic Welfare*, pp. 316, 317.

41. Clark Kerr, "The Prospect for Wages and Hours in 1975," in Jack Stieber, ed., *U.S. Industrial Relations: The Next Twenty Years* (East Lansing: Michigan State University Press, 1958), pp. 167–194; Pryor, *Property and Industrial Organization*, table 3–3, p. 78.

42. Alex Inkeles and Peter H. Rossi, "National Comparisons of Occupational Prestige," *American Journal of Sociology* 61 (January 1956): 329–339.

43. "Rethinking Engineers' Training, Status," translation and summary of several articles, in *The Current Digest of the Soviet Press* 53 (July 8, 1981): 1–3, 20.

44. Harold Wilensky, *The Welfare State and Equality* (Berkeley: University of California Press, 1975).

45. Gregory and Stuart, *Comparative Economic Systems*, p. 393.

46. Karl Marx, *Capital*, vol. 3, *The Process of Capitalist Production as a Whole*, ed. Friedrich Engels (New York: International Publishers, 1967; orig. pub. 1894), p. 388.

47. Adrian Karatnycky, Alexander J. Motyl, and Adolph Sturmthal, *Workers' Rights, East and West* (New Brunswick, N.J.: Transaction Books, 1980).

48. Dunlop, *Industrial Relations Systems*, ch. 1.

49. Frederic L. Pryor, *Public Expenditures in Communist and Capitalist Nations* (Homewood, Ill.: Richard D. Irwin, 1968), pp. 310, 285, 282.

50. Irma Adelman and Cynthia Taft Morris, *Economic Growth and Social Equity in Developing Countries* (Stanford: Stanford University Press, 1973), p. 139.

51. Karl Marx, *The Eighteenth Brumaire of Louis Bonaparte* (New York: International Publishers, 1935; orig. pub. 1852), p. 13.

52. Alfred Marshall, *Principles of Economics*, 3rd ed., vol. 1 (London: Macmillan, 1895), p. 1.

53. Edward Shils, *Tradition* (Chicago: University of Chicago Press, 1981), pp. 295ff. See pp. 291–295 for Max Weber's views on convergence through the process of rationalization.

54. Chenery and Syrquin, *Patterns of Development*.

55. Gregory and Stuart, *Comparative Economic Systems*, p. 406.

56. Alex Inkeles, "Industrial Man: The Relation of Status to Experience, Perception, and Value," *American Journal of Sociology* 66 (July 1960): 1–31; Alex Inkeles and David H. Smith, *Becoming Modern: Individual Change in Six Developing Countries* (Cambridge, Mass.: Harvard University Press, 1974), p. 6; Alex Inkeles, "Convergence and Divergence in Industrial Societies," program report no. 80-B3, April 1980, Institute for Research on Educational Finance and Governance, School of Education, Stanford University (IFG), p. 18.

57. Kirschen, ed., *Economic Policies Compared*, vol. 1, p. 291.

58. Stephen Jay Kobrin, *Foreign Direct Investment, Industrialization and Social Change: Acculturation and Modernization in Developing Countries* (diss., University of Michigan, 1975), p. 183.

59. Thorkil Kristensen, *Development in Rich and Poor Countries: A General Theory with Statistical Analyses* (New York: Praeger, 1974), pp. 137, 111.

60. Simon Kuznets, *Six Lectures on Economic Growth* (Glencoe, Ill.: Free Press, 1959), p. 111; idem, *Modern Economic Growth: Rate, Structure, and Spread* (New Haven: Yale University Press, 1966), pp. 447, 452; idem, *Economic Growth of Nations* (Cambridge, Mass.: Harvard University Press, 1971), p. 348.

61. Friedrich Engels, Letter to Karl Marx, 1868, in *Karl Marx and Friedrich Engels on Britain* (Moscow, 1953), pp. 499–500; quoted in Robert McKenzie and Allan Silver, *Angels in Marble: Working Class Conservatives in Urban England* (London: Heinemann, 1968), p. 14. Karl Marx and Friedrich Engels, *Selected Correspondence, 1846–1895*, tr. Dona Torr (New York: International Publishers, 1942), pp. 355–356, letter from Marx to Wilhelm Liebknecht, February 1878.

62. John Goldthorpe, "Social Stratification in Industrial Society," in Paul Halmos, ed., *The Development of Industrial Societies*, monograph no. 8 of *Sociological Review* (Keele: University of Keele, 1964), p. 197; and idem, *Social Mobility and Class Structure in Modern Britain* (Oxford: Clarendon Press, 1980), p. 273. See also Michael Mann, *Consciousness and Action among the Western Working Class* (London: Macmillan, 1973).

63. T. H. Marshall, "A Summing Up," in Halmos, ed., *The Development of Industrial Societies*, pp. 144–145.

64. James C. Abegglen, *The Japanese Factory: Aspects of Its Social Organization* (Glencoe, Ill.: Free Press, 1958). Abegglen believes that "the assumption of similarity in organizational systems and in relationships in industry is in error" (p. 7). "The Japanese case suggests that these experiences and the organizational system used in the West are not necessary to the introduction of industry into another social system" (p. 131).

65. Organisation for Economic Co-operation and Development, *The Development of Industrial Relations Systems: Some Implications of Japanese Experience* (Paris: OECD, 1977).

66. Ronald Dore, *Human Resources Research*, ed. John Oxenham, Institute of Development Studies Bulletin, February 1975, University of Sussex, England, p. 33. See also idem, *British Factory, Japanese Factory* (London: Allen & Unwin, 1973). Dore found "radical differences" between the two types of factory situations, but he also noted a common tendency toward "organization-oriented" forms of work organization and away from "market-oriented forms" (pp. 11–12).

67. Robert E. Cole, *Work, Mobility, and Participation: A Comparative Study of American and Japanese Industry* (Berkeley: University of California Press, 1979), p. 10.

68. Kazuo Okochi, Bernard Karsh, and Solomon B. Levine, eds., *Workers and Employers in Japan: The Japanese Employment Relations System* (Princeton, N.J.: Princeton University Press, 1974), p. 505.

69. Robert M. Marsh and Hiroshi Mannari, *Modernization and the Japanese Factory* (Princeton, N.J.: Princeton University Press, 1976), p. 338.

70. Edwin O. Reischauer, *The Japanese* (Cambridge, Mass.: Harvard University Press, 1977), p. 123.

71. Ichiro Nakayama, *Industrialization and Labor-Management Relations in Japan* (Tokyo: Japan Institute of Labor, 1975), pp. 36, 38, 40, 86.

72. J. Hirschmeier and T. Yui, *The Development of Japanese Business, 1600–1980*, 2nd ed. (London: Allen & Unwin, 1981), p. 11.

73. Tadashi Hanami, *Labor Relations in Japan Today* (Tokyo: Kodansha International, 1979), p. 236.

74. Ibid., p. 15.

75. S. Takezawa and A. M. Whitehill, *Work Ways: Japan and America* (Tokyo: Japan Institute of Labor, 1981), p. 178.

76. Christopher Howe, *Wage Patterns and Wage Policy in Modern China, 1919–1972* (New York: Cambridge University Press, 1973).

77. Paul M. Sweezy and Charles Bettelheim, *On the Transition to Socialism* (New York: Monthly Review Press, 1971), p. 4.

78. Georg W. F. Hegel, *The Philosophy of History*, tr. J. Sibree (New York: Dover, 1956; lectures originally given c. 1830), p. 19.

79. Szczepański, "Early Stages," p. 13.

3. The Near Future of Industrial Societies

1. Karl Popper, *The Open Society and Its Enemies*, vol. 2, *The High Tide of Prophecy: Hegel, Marx, and the Aftermath* (London: Routledge & Kegan Paul, 1945), pp. 254–256. See also the discussion in Popper, *The Poverty of Historicism* (Boston: Beacon Press, 1957).

2. Robert Aaron Gordon, "Institutional Elements in Contemporary Economics," in *Institutional Economics: Veblen, Commons, and Mitchell Reconsidered*, a series of lectures by Joseph Dorfman, C. E. Ayres, Neil W. Chamberlain, Simon Kuznets, and R. A. Gordon (Berkeley: University of California Press, 1964), p. 147.

3. Arthur M. Okun, *Equality and Efficiency: The Big Trade Off* (Washington, D.C.: Brookings Institution, 1975), p. 120. See also Ellman's discussion of the views of J. van den Doel that "different economic systems have different objectives," in Michael Ellman, "Against Convergence," *Cambridge Journal of Economics* 4 (September 1980):201.

4. Janos Kornai, "The Dilemmas of a Socialist Economy," *Cambridge Journal of Economics* 4 (June 1980): 147–157.

5. Alexis de Tocqueville, *Democracy in America*, tr. Henry Reeve (London: Oxford University Press, 1965; orig. pub. 1835), p. 431.

6. Friedrich Engels, *The Origin of the Family, Private Property*

and the State, quoted in Alexander Gray, *The Socialist Tradition: Moses to Lenin,* 2nd ed. (London: Longmans, Green, 1947; orig. pub. in German, 1884).

7. The estimate of 12 million products is from Alec Nove, "The Security Complex of the Soviet Union," *Times Higher Education Supplement,* October 17, 1980, p. 11.

8. Gregory Grossman, "Notes on the Illegal Private Economy and Corruption," Joint Economic Committee, *Soviet Economy in a Time of Change,* vol. 1, 96th Congress, 1st sess. (Washington, D.C.: Government Printing Office, 1979), pp. 834–855. Grossman uses the term "second economy" to include both legal and illegal activities outside the plan. The present text makes a distinction between the second economy of legal activities which are outside the plan, and the third economy of illegal or corrupt activities. The statement in the text that the second economy is growing is based on personal interviews by Clark Kerr in the USSR in the fall of 1981.

9. Adolph A. Berle, Jr., and Gardiner C. Means, *The Modern Corporation and Private Property* (New York: Macmillan, 1933), pp. 119, 3.

10. Joseph A. Schumpeter, *Capitalism, Socialism, and Democracy* (New York: Harper, 1942; 3rd ed., 1950), p. 168.

11. Ibid., p. 419; Sumner H. Slichter, "Are We Becoming a 'Laboristic' State?" in John T. Dunlop, ed., *Potentials of the American Economy: Selected Essays of Sumner H. Slichter* (Cambridge, Mass.: Harvard University Press, 1961), p. 255.

12. H. Linnemann, J. P. Pronk, and J. Tinbergen, "Convergence of Economic Systems in East and West," in Morris Bornstein and Daniel Fusfeld, eds., *The Soviet Economy: A Book of Readings,* 3rd ed. (Homewood, Ill.: Richard D. Irwin, 1970). Others who share this view include:

Abram Bergson: "The two systems . . . have evolved in the course of time and we are certainly not quite so dissimilar as the alternatives Marx depicted. In future they may converge still more." Bergson, *Planning and Productivity under Soviet Socialism* (New York: Columbia University Press, 1968), p. 73.

Alexander Eckstein: "This does not mean that economic institutions are uniquely predetermined by a particular type of technology; rather it defines a circumscribed range of possibilities." Eckstein, "Economic Development and Political Change in Communist Systems," *World Politics* 22 (July 1970): 476.

Gregory Grossman: "Industrialization and its concomitants . . .

impose their stamp on outlooks, values, behavior patterns, and even forms of economic organization," but major differences remain. Grossman, *Economic Systems*, 2nd ed. (Englewood Cliffs, N.J.: Prentice-Hall, 1974), p. 177.

Robert Heilbroner: "What seems to impend at the moment, then, is a *convergence of economic mechanisms* for the more advanced societies." But "this does not imply that the two major systems today are about to become indistinguishable." Heilbroner, *The Making of Economic Society* (Englewood Cliffs, N.J.: Prentice-Hall, 1968), p. 219.

But see also the view of Peter Wiles that "the Soviet-type system will not greatly change." He calls the view that there will be a convergence "on an optimum society" the "Dutch Economist's Disease." Wiles, "A Sovietological View," in Arnold Heertje, ed., *Schumpeter's Vision* (New York: Praeger, 1981), pp. 164 and 168.

13. E. S. Kirschen, ed., *Economic Policies Compared, West and East*, vol. 1 (Amsterdam: North-Holland, 1974), pp. 336–337.

14. Nick Eberstadt, "The Health Crisis in the USSR," *New York Review of Books* 28 (February 19, 1981): 23–31, a review of Christopher Davis and Murray Feshbach, *Rising Infant Mortality in the USSR in the 1970s*, U.S. Bureau of the Census, ser. P-95, no. 74 (Washington, D.C.: Government Printing Office, September 1980). Also see Vladimir G. Treml, "Death from Alcohol Poisoning in the USSR," *Wall Street Journal*, November 10, 1981, p. 23.

15. Abram Bergson, "Soviet Economic Slowdown and the 1981–85 Plan," *Problems of Communism* 30 (May–June 1981): p. 33.

16. See discussion in Adam B. Ulam, *Russia's Failed Revolution* (New York: Basic Books, 1981), p. 429.

17. George Konrad and Ivan Szelényi, *The Intellectuals on the Road to Class Power*, tr. Andrew Arato and Richard E. Allen (New York: Harcourt Brace Jovanovitch, 1979), p. 209.

18. Jerry F. Hough, *Soviet Leadership in Transition* (Washington, D.C.: Brookings Institution, 1980), table 2-5, p. 28.

19. The concept of a "new class" or of new classes is a slippery one. See the discussion in Frederic L. Pryor, "The 'New Class': Analysis of the Concept, the Hypothesis and the Idea as a Research Tool," *American Journal of Economics and Sociology* 40 (October 1981): 367–379.

20. Milovan Djilas, *The New Class: An Analysis of the Communist System* (London: Thames and Hudson, 1957).

21. Irma Adelman and Cynthia Taft Morris, "A Factor Analysis

of the Interrelationship Between Social and Political Variables and Per Capita Gross National Product," *Quarterly Journal of Economics* 79 (November 1965): 555–578.

22. Karl Marx, *The Civil War in France* (New York: International Publishers, 1940), p. 57, originally an address to the General Council of the First International, May 30, 1871.

23. Leszek Kolakowski, *Main Currents of Marxism: Its Rise, Growth, and Dissolution*, vol. 2, *The Golden Age*, tr. from the Polish by P. S. Falla (Oxford: Clarendon Press, 1978), pp. 480, 488, 503, 505, 507. Lenin also claimed that "the history of all countries shows that the working class, solely by its own forces, is able to work out merely trade-union consciousness." V. I. Lenin, *What is To Be Done? Burning Questions of Our Movement* (Oxford: Clarendon Press, 1963; orig. pub. 1902), p. 63.

24. Leon Trotsky, *The Defence of Terrorism: A Reply to Karl Kautsky* (London: Allen & Unwin, 1935; orig. pub. 1921 as *Terrorism and Communism*), pp. 102, 127.

25. Quoted in Kazimierz Slomczyński and Tadeusz Krauze, eds., *Class Structure and Social Mobility in Poland* (White Plains, N.Y.: M. E. Sharpe, 1978), p. ix. See also Jan Szczepański, "La Société industrielle socialiste," in *Mélanges en l'honneur de Raymond Aron* (Paris: Calman-Levy,1971). He states here that convergence between socialism and capitalism will take a long time, if it ever occurs at all. Many vested interests, including the new group of technocrats, support the essence of socialism, which is political control by the party and economic control by the plan. Socialism will evolve and change in many ways but remain different from neocapitalist societies.

26. Sidney Hook, "Evolution in Communism?" in *Revolution, Reform and Social Justice: Studies in the Theory and Practice of Marxism* (New York: New York University Press, 1975), p. 177.

27. Karl Marx and Friedrich Engels, *Manifesto of the Communist Party* (orig. pub. 1848), in Robert C. Tucker, ed., *The Marx-Engels Reader*, 2nd ed. (New York: Norton, 1978), pp. 500, 491. The phrase "dictatorship of the proletariat" was used by Marx in a letter to Joseph Weydemeyer, March 5, 1852, ibid., p. 220.

28. "Marxism . . . has been but an ideological façade in the country where it originally triumphed . . . Marxism as well as the bourgeoisie . . . produces its own gravediggers." Adam B. Ulam, *The Unfinished Revolution* (Boulder, Colo.: Westview Press, 1979), p. 276.

29. Robert Michels, *Political Parties: A Sociological Study of*

the Oligarchical Tendencies of Modern Democracy (Glencoe, Ill.: Free Press, 1958; orig. pub. 1915), pp. 418, 393.

30. Berle and Means, *Modern Corporation*, p. 2.

31. Hook, "Evolution in Communism," p. 181.

32. Contrasting views include:

Zbigniew Brzezinski and Samuel P. Huntington: "The Soviet and the American political systems, each in its own way, have been highly successful. Because they have been successful, they are not likely to change drastically . . . The evolution of the two systems, but not their convergence, seems to be the undramatic pattern for the future." Brzezinski and Huntington, *Political Power, USA/USSR* (New York: Viking, 1964), p. 436.

S. Gomulka: "The prospects for democratization in Eastern Europe must in my view remain poor." Gomulka, "Economic Factors in the Democratization of Socialism and the Socialization of Capitalism," *Journal of Comparative Economics* 1 (December 1977): 406.

P. J. D. Wiles: "There will, furthermore, be no convergence in political systems . . . Power is wielded within any nation state according to its traditions and to historical chance. Imitation of other countries plays a small part, invasion by them a larger one. But the relations between the political and the economic set-up are extremely loose." Wiles, *Economic Institutions Compared* (Oxford: Basil Blackwell, 1977), p. 543. But he does note that "the Party, too, of course, is converging," becoming more bureaucratic, less revolutionary (p. 545).

W. Brus: Convergence on both market socialism and political democracy is needed in order to get greater economic efficiency. Brus, *Social Ownership and Political Systems* (London: Routledge & Kegan Paul, 1975).

Issac Deutscher: Russia will move toward a "socialist democracy" with an end of terror, a reduction of the cult of personality, more free discussion within the party, and more affluent and less fearful citizens. Deutscher, *Russia: What Next?* (Oxford: Oxford University Press, 1953), pp. 208, 221–230.

Alexander Eckstein: "There is a significant degree of correlation between economic and political change . . . Consequently, the totalitarian features of Communist systems may become transformed and alleviated in the process of economic growth. This need not imply the advent of democracy nor the withering away of Communist dictatorships, but rather a change in their form." Eckstein, *Comparison of Economic Systems: Theoretical and Methodological*

Approaches (Berkeley: University of California Press, 1971), pp. 475, 495.

Branko Horvat: In the "étatist nations, one can expect a relaxation of political coercion and the development of more humane relationships." Horvat, *The Political Economy of Socialism* (Armonk, N.Y.: M. E. Sharpe, 1982), p. 55.

33. W. Averell Harriman, *Special Envoy: 1941–1946* (New York: Random House, 1975), p. vi.

34. Paul M. Sweezy, *Post-Revolutionary Society* (New York: Monthly Review Press, 1980), pp. 147–151.

35. Simon Kuznets, *Modern Economic Growth: Rate, Structure, and Spread* (New Haven: Yale University Press, 1966), p. 508.

36. Fred Hirsch, *The Social Limits to Growth* (Cambridge, Mass.: Harvard University Press, 1976), pp. 1, 3, 7.

37. Daniel Bell, *The Cultural Contradictions of Capitalism* (New York: Basic Books, 1976).

38. Arthur Koestler et al., with introd. by Richard Crossman, *The God That Failed: Six Studies in Communism* (London: Hamish Hamilton, 1950).

4. A New Stage of History?

1. Herman Kahn and John B. Phelps, "The Economic Present and Future," *Futurist* 13 (June 1979):202–222; Richard A. Falk, *This Endangered Planet: Prospects and Proposals for Human Survival* (New York: Random House, 1971), ch. 9.

2. Wassily Leontief, *The Future of the World Economy: A United Nations Study* (New York: Oxford University Press, 1977); Organisation for Economic Co-operation and Development, *Facing the Future: Mastering the Probable and Managing the Unpredictable*, Interfutures (Paris: OECD, 1979); *The Global 2000 Report to the President: Entering the Twenty-First Century* (Washington, D.C.: Government Printing Office, 1980); Eric Ashby, "A Second Look at Doom," Fawley Foundation Lecture, University of Southampton (England), 1975, p. 17.

3. See Franz Kafka, *The Trial* (New York: Modern Library, 1956; orig. pub. in German, 1925), among other works by Kafka; George Orwell, *1984* (New York: Harcourt, Brace, 1949); Aldous Huxley, *Brave New World: A Novel* (New York: Harper, 1946).

4. Michael Boretsky, "The Role of Innovation," *Challenge* 23 (November–December 1980): 9–15. See also the discussion in Mensch: "Since the mid-1960s, symptoms of stagnation in the

Western industrial nations have become increasingly evident; very few basic innovations were implemented in the years between 1953 and 1973. Moreover, the stream of improvement innovations in established areas of the economy has dwindled, producing progressively fewer useful ideas and being infiltrated by pseudo-innovations." Gerhard Mensch, *Stalemate in Technology: Innovations Overcome the Depression* (Cambridge, Mass.: Ballinger, 1979; orig. pub. in German, 1975), p. 86.

5. Kenneth Boulding, *Ecodynamics* (New York: Sage Publications, 1978), pp. 224, 327.

6. Thorkil Kristensen notes how growth tends to be "slow during the earlier parts of the process"; then it moves "faster"; and this is followed by a "slow down because a stage will have been reached at which existing knowledge is already utilized to a large extent." He goes on to say that if the level of knowledge "were constant over a long period," production per capita would "gradually approach a ceiling determined by the level of existing knowledge." However, even if the level of knowledge keeps on rising, developed countries would still grow at a slower rate than developing countries because they would be at the frontiers of knowledge and not catching up with these frontiers. Thus, we have an "S-shaped" growth curve. Kristensen, *Development in Rich and Poor Countries: A General Theory with Statistical Analyses* (New York: Praeger, 1974), pp. 26, 28, 29. See also W. W. Rostow, *Why the Poor Get Richer and the Rich Slow Down* (Austin: University of Texas Press, 1980), pp. 275ff.

7. Robert Heilbroner, "Some Second Thoughts on *The Human Prospect*," *Challenge* 18 (May–June 1975): 25.

8. Zbigniew M. Fallenbuchl, "Poland: Command Planning in Crisis," *Challenge* 24 (July–August 1981): 5–12. Also see idem, "The Polish Economy at the Beginning of the 1980's," in *Poland, 1980: An East European Country Study*, a collection of papers submitted to the U.S. Congress, Joint Economic Committee, September 1, 1980.

9. Herman Kahn and Thomas Pepper, *The Japanese Challenge* (New York: Thomas Y. Crowell, 1979), pp. 144–145. For a discussion of Karl Marx's view of the "Asiatic mode of production," see Lawrence Krader, *The Asiatic Mode of Production: Sources, Development and Critique on the Writings of Karl Marx* (Assen, Netherlands: Van Gorcum, 1975), esp. chs. 2 and 7. Marx wrote of the "communal" orientation of production.

10. Robert E. Cole, *Work, Mobility, and Participation: A Com-*

parative Study of American and Japanese Industry (Berkeley: University of California Press, 1979), pp. 222–223.

11. See, for example, Richard Tanner Pascale and Anthony G. Athos, *The Art of Japanese Management: Applications for American Executives* (New York: Simon and Schuster, 1981).

12. Edwin O. Reischauer, *The Japanese* (Cambridge, Mass.: Harvard University Press, 1977), p. 194.

13. Marquis Childs, *Sweden: The Middle Way* (New Haven: Yale University Press, 1936). Sweden and other northwestern European countries may again show the way, in the view of Jan Sollenius. See Sollenius, *Functional Evolutionary Materialism* (Stockholm: Swedish Institute of Social Research, 1982).

14. Ralf Dahrendorf, "The Politics of Economic Decline," *Political Studies* 29 (June 1981): 284–291.

15. James E. Alt, *The Politics of Economic Decline: Economic Management and Political Behaviour in Britain since 1964* (Cambridge: Cambridge University Press, 1979), pp. 258, 270, 273. For a contrary view, see Charles F. Carter, "Future Darkness," *Science and Public Policy* 1 (June 1974): 99–100. Possibly even in Britain, "dictatorship" will be accepted as growth rates decline and then turn negative.

16. Sidney and Beatrice Webb, *Soviet Communism: A New Civilization?* (London: Longman's, Green, 1935). They end with the question, "Will it spread?"; they reply, "Yes, it will" (p. 1143).

17. Ezra F. Vogel, *Japan as Number One: Lessons for America* (Cambridge, Mass.: Harvard University Press, 1979).

18. E. J. Mishan, *The Economic Growth Debate: An Assessment* (London: Allen & Unwin, 1977), p. 266.

19. For a discussion of a three-way split into the "New Right" with its emphasis on law and order and on low taxes, the "New Left" with its emphasis on equality of results and on participative democracy, and the "counterculture" with its emphasis on no growth and on new life styles, see Ralf Dahrendorf, *After Social Democracy* (London: Liberal Publication Department, 1980), pp. 10–12.

20. *The Youth of the World and Japan: The Findings of the Second World Youth Survey* (Tokyo: Youth Bureau, Prime Minister's Office, 1978), p. 24.

21. V. I. Lenin, Speech of December 6, 1920, in *Collected Works*, vol. 31 (London: Lawrence & Wishart, 1960–1970), p. 457.

22. Karl W. Deutsch, "Social and Political Convergence in Industrializing Countries," in Nancy Hammond, ed., *Social Science*

in New Societies: Problems in Cross-Cultural Research and Theory Building (Ann Arbor: Social Science Research Bureau, University of Michigan, 1973), p. 105.

23. Zbigniew Brzezinski and Samuel P. Huntington, *Political Power, USA/USSR* (New York: Viking, 1964), p. 429.

24. Falk, *Endangered Planet*, p. 436.

25. Harlan Cleveland, *The Third Try at World Order* (Philadelphia: World Affairs Council of Philadelphia, 1976).

26. Willy Brandt, *North-South: A Program for Survival* (Cambridge, Mass.: MIT Press, 1980).

27. Simon Kuznets, *Modern Economic Growth: Rate, Structure, and Spread* (New Haven: Yale University Press, 1966).

28. Kahn and Pepper, *Japanese Challenge*, p. 6.

29. Bertrand Russell, in collaboration with Dora Russell, *The Prospects of Industrial Civilization* (New York: Century, 1923), Preface.

30. See the discussion in Tibor Scitovsky, *The Joyless Economy: An Inquiry into Human Satisfaction and Consumer Dissatisfaction* (New York: Oxford University Press, 1976).

Selected Bibliography

Bornstein, Morris. "East European Economic Reforms and the Convergence of Economic Systems." *Jahrbuch der Wirtschaft Osteuropas*, vol. 2. Munich: Gunter Olzog Verlag, 1971, pp. 247–267. Bornstein analyzes the theoretical foundations of the convergence hypothesis and finds some empirical evidence of convergence in changes that took place in East European countries in the 1960s.

Dunning, E. G., and E. I. Hopper. "Industrialization and the Problem of Convergence." *Sociological Review*, n.s. 14 (July 1966): 163–186. Dunning and Hopper provide a review of much of the American literature on convergence written in the early 1960s.

Ellman, Michael. "Against Convergence." *Cambridge Journal of Economics* 4 (September 1980): 199–210. Ellman mainly discusses convergence theory as set forth by Tinbergen and his followers, including J. van den Doel. The article includes a review of the literature in Dutch.

Goldthorpe, John H. "Theories of Industrial Society." *Archives*

Européennes de Sociologie 12, no. 2 (1971): 263–288. Goldthorpe provides a critical review of *Industrialism and Industrial Man*.

Gouré, Leon, Foy D. Kohler, Richard Soll, and Annette Stiefbold. *Convergence of Communism and Capitalism: The Soviet View*. Miami: Center for Advanced International Studies, University of Miami, 1973. The best review of Soviet literature.

Kernig, C. D., ed. "Convergence." In *Marxism, Communism, and Western Society*. New York: Herder and Herder, 1972, pp. 210–216. This is an encyclopedia-type article that includes a review of some Soviet as well as Western literature on convergence up to the late 1960s.

Lauterbach, Albert. "The 'Convergence' Controversy Revisited." *Kyklos* 29 (1976): 733–754. Lauterbach reviews various forms the convergence debate has taken. The article includes a review of the literature in German.

Lipset, Seymour Martin. "The End of Ideology and the Ideology of the Intellectuals." In Joseph Ben-David and Terry Nichols Clark, *Culture and Its Creators*. Chicago: University of Chicago Press, 1977, pp. 15–42. Lipset provides a sympathetic review of the "end of ideology" literature.

Meyer, Alfred G. "Theories of Convergence." In Chalmers Johnson, ed., *Change in Communist Systems*. Stanford, Calif.: Stanford University Press, 1970, pp. 313–341. Meyer reviews convergence theory, especially in the United States, in the 1950s and 1960s.

Meyer, John W., John Boli-Bennett, and Christopher Chase-Dunn. "Convergence and Divergence in Development." In Alex Inkeles, ed., *Annual Review of Sociology*, vol. 1 (Palo Alto: Annual Reviews, Inc., 1975), pp. 223–246.

Millar, James R. "On the Theory and Measurement of Convergence." In Morris Bornstein, ed., *Comparative Economic Systems: Models and Cases*, 3rd ed. Homewood, Ill.: Richard D. Irwin, 1974, pp. 481–492. This is a critical review paying particular attention to Karl Marx's *Capital*; John Hicks's *A Theory of Economic History*, in which he postulates convergence around "the rise of the market"; and Clarence Ayres's *Theory of Economic Progress*, with its emphasis on technological imperatives as a force in economic change.

Pryor, Frederic L. *Property and Industrial Organization in Communist and Capitalist Nations*. Bloomington: Indiana University Press, 1973, pp. 356–371. Pryor reviews arguments for and against convergence.

Spulber, Nicholas. "Socialism, Industrialization and 'Convergence.'" *Jahrbuch der Wirtschaft Osteuropas*, vol. 2. Munich: Gunter Olzog Verlag, 1971, pp. 397–424. This study examines definitions of modern socialism, and identifies institutions and structures common to all industrialized nations, socialist and capitalist.

Spulber, Nicolas, and Ira Horowitz. "Convergence Theories and Optimal Systems." In Spulber and Horowitz, *Quantitative Economic Policy and Planning: Theory and Models of Economic Control*. New York: Norton, 1976, ch. 18, pp. 367–391. The authors review theories of economic convergence, concentrating on those of Tinbergen, Galbraith, and Rostow.

Waxman, Chaim I., ed. *The End of Ideology Debate*. New York: Funk & Wagnalls, 1968. Waxman has edited and written an introduction to a collection of selections from major participants in the debate, mainly in the United States, from 1955 to 1968.

Weinberg, Ian. "The Problem of the Convergence of Industrial Societies: A Critical Look at the State of a Theory." *Comparative Studies in Society and History* 11 (January 1969): 1–15. Weinberg notes the remnants of eighteenth- and nineteenth-century theories of progress in present-day modernization theory in the form of theories of convergence on an optimum. He reviews current literature, mostly American and based on functionalist positions.

Index